NihONSENSE

by Paul Meredith Stuart

The **Japan Times**, Ltd.

NihONSENSE
© Copyright 1987 by Paul Meredith Stuart
All rights reserved.

First printing: May 1987
Sixth printing: August 1989

Photograph on p. 55: M. Naka; others, S.A. Atkin
Illustration: M.K. Hazelrigg
Cover design: Atelier Hirata

Published by The Japan Times
5-4, Shibaura 4-chome, Minato-ku, Tokyo 108, Japan

Printed in Japan.
ISBN4-7890-0349-3 C0095

FOREWORD

Explaining Japan and the Japanese is big these days.

There are Japanese who specialize in explaining themselves to themselves, and have built up a cozy little subject called *nihonjin-ron* — but nothing to do with the American president called Ron who tried so hard to understand Japan in the 1980s. The *nihonjin-ron* seems to consist mostly of attempts to congratulate the Japanese on being Japanese, but there are those who seek to spread the word to non-Japanese, too. They usually end in failure, with an exasperated and exasperating, "You don't understand, because you aren't Japanese." But if Japanese civilization really is so unique, why does it claim to be so, just like every other nation, race, region, cult, sect and clique in the world? How many Chosen Peoples can the world hold?

Then there are foreigners who come to Japan for a couple of weeks and on their return home, like the one-eyed man in the land of the blind, become instant experts in the country and its food, language, industrial relations, ancient history, scenic beauty, attitude to religion, political philosophy, etc., etc., etc. It's difficult to say who does more damage.

This book stands back, takes a cool look at all sorts of things that happen in Japanese society, and discovers that most of the attempts to explain them are, quite simply, funny. Usually unintentionally funny, which is dangerous. Indeed, the things that happen are funny themselves.

In the words of the proverbs, there's many a true word spoken in jest, and if the cap fits, wear it.

Robert Burns wrote:

> *O wad some Pow'r the giftie gie us*
> *To see oursels as others see us!*
> *It wad frae mony a blunder free us*
> *And foolish notion.*

And Dryden or Pope or Byron or somebody like that wrote of satire soothing with morals what it hurts with wit.

Now, to what extent do these apply to this book? How much of it is in jest, and how many of those jests bear any truth? Does the author want the Japanese people to wear a hat that he places on their heads, or has he unwittingly fitted his own head into a cap that might even turn into a noose? Does this book really tell Japanese people very much about how others see them? Does it present any morals, or any wit for that matter? Is any pain caused, and if so, is it soothed?

What a lot of questions! And not a single answer! For the answers are up to readers to decide. They may recognize an experience of their own, and then either approve or disapprove of its treatment here. They may find parts of the book cruel, or silly, or shallow, or just in general too exaggerated for their taste. But the author does hope that it will provide them with some food for thought beyond the first giggle, or the first fit of anger in which the book is flung violently away against the cockroach trap. Thank God few Japanese homes have open fires.

The author has, after all, observed, experienced and overheard quite a lot about living in Japan. He has been confused, enlightened, enraged and delighted just like everybody else. Readers are welcome to react similarly to the book, too, but it is to be hoped that they will not be delighted only by those parts in which they are not being made fun of themselves, nor will be enraged at those parts where they feel themselves directly under attack. It is that attitude that is surely the funniest of all. Remember Robert Burns and the well-fitting cap.

So much of modern Japanese life is depressingly similar to modern life anywhere else in the world. What overseas visitors notice first is the differences — and often the unpleasant differences. The Japan Times, it is true, frequently runs readers' letters about how clean, honest and polite the Japanese are, and it would have been nice to produce a book about that. But as any J.T. journalist will tell you, without fear or favor, it's the dirtiness, dishonesty and rudeness in life that makes news. So in these pages you will mostly find the Japanese being dirty, dishonest and rude, but please, please remember that they aren't like that all the time. Nor are they always inscrutable, or unpredictable, but who ever got a good story out of scrutability and predictability?

The term ''economic animal'' was coined as one of contempt, but taken up by many Japanese at the time as a compliment. So it may be that something in these pages intended as a savage attack will be taken as fulsome praise; on the other hand, something only intended as a weak, silly joke may be seen by more (or less) perceptive readers as vicious, nasty prejudice. If the cap fits, ...

A nation where taxi-drivers religiously give you back ¥10 in change but politicians and industrialists exchange bribes in the high millions, where men use the street as their toilet but carefully wipe their hands afterwards, where wives are downtrodden but often have full control of their husband's pay packet, and where children are spoon-fed and mollycoddled but forced to attend cram schools for hours every evening — such a nation can't help being funny. In any case, it's all NihONSENSE.

Paul Meredith Stuart
April 1987

CONTENTS

I
Them and Us

Why "International"?

The more often you say it, the more likely you are to believe it. If the prime minister goes to a department store and pays ten times the normal price for a golf shirt just because it's from Europe, you think he must be crazy; but if he then tells you that he's being "international" by doing so, you admire him and respect him for being such a fine person and so, well, what better praise than to call him a true internationalist? Call something international, and its value doubles. Its price usually goes up by much more than that.

Often, of course, as everybody has noticed, things are called international in reverse proportion to how international they really are. The airports of Paris, Rome, London don't call themselves "International," although it would not be surprising to hear that an actual majority of their flights serve other countries. But any Japanese provincial airfield that once arranged for a charter flight to take local agricultural cooperative members on a sex tour to a nearby Asian nation immediately has the right, nay, obligation to call itself proudly an International Airport. An International Golf Club may have as its only claim to internationalism that it employs cheap, illegal foreign labor for its bar staff. There is a bus company with "International" in its name that serves an area within 20 km or so of Ikebukuro. Aren't foreigners refused service in some of the bars on Kobe's Kokusai-dōri (International Avenue)?

And the more the word is used, the more each individual

begins to worry whether he himself is as internationalized as he ought to be. He goes to lecture meetings on "How to Be Internationalized" by students from the American Midwest who had never been beyond their local bus depot before they suddenly found themselves in Japan expected to perform as grand gurus on all aspects of internationalization. He takes a package tour to Hawaii, staying in a hotel run by a large Japanese chain and providing Japanese meals three times a day. He copies the prime minister and buys foreign clothes, thereby bankrupting himself and lining the pockets of the Japanese importers.

But all the time he didn't really need to worry. The Japanese are already international. Whether they use the word or not. They are all of mixed blood. They all learn a foreign language at school. They all eat food that is imported, whether they know it or not. They all . . . . Complete the list with ten other items of evidence that the Japanese are international, from your own experience, hearsay, or prejudice.

So we come back to the original question. Why is that word so damn popular? Why can't people give up being so neurotic about it and just accept that everybody in Japan is already internationalized? Only when that happens will everybody really be internationalized.

Why "Americans"?

To many Japanese, all foreigners are "Americans." "I know," you may be anticipating, "you're gonna say we all

look alike to them! But it's the Japanese who look alike —
or at least wanna look alike." You've obviously been
around and you have some insight into the Japanese mentality, but the reason is not quite so simple and the reality
is that not all foreigners are *gaijin* to Japanese and quite a
few natives of Japan are *gaijin!* There is a logic to this mess,
but it is hardly logical.

It is true that "American" *(Amerikajin)* is a synonym for
gaijin for many Japanese. At one time, at least when the
U.S. auto industry was undisputed leader of world
autodom, the term connoted awe and respect. But certainly
not to most Europeans or citizens of American states north
(Canada) and south (from Mexico to the Falklands) of the
United States. Most, including a few sensitive U.S.
citizens, can only resent being so stereotyped. From the
Vietnam War era to the present day, "Americans" still
come off as the ugly American: boorish, uncultured,
money-flashing/-grubbing, monolingual impertinents;
potential drug-fiends, CIA agents or both. (Never mind
that they are generous, friendly, honest, helpful and so
individualistic as to defy all stereotyping.) Japanese,
however, do not apply the word *gaijin* to all foreigners. In
fact, it doesn't even apply to all "Americans"!

Asians, for example, are *Indojin* (Indians), *Chūgokujin*
(Chinese), *Chōsenjin* (Koreans — disregarding political
realities of north and south which prevent the use of the
term in broadcasting) and so on for most non-Europeans of
color. None of these terms carry connotations of respect,
although nearly all are the historical and cultural superiors
of Japan in the same way Europe is to the U.S.

In spite of the fashionable popularity blacks enjoy among the young-at-heart Japanese, *kokujin* (Negroes, Blacks) still connotes the contempt Japanese learned from the Black Americans' fellow Occupation personnel or that was otherwise retained from Japanese chauvinism toward Melanesians and Africans as reinforced by Nazism.

In short, to the majority of Japanese, *gaijin* means *hakujin* (white men, whites, Caucasians, in that order) and seldom applies to people of color. The misapplication of *amerikajin* simply guarantees insult to a good many whites as well.

Of course, legal usage of the term *gaijin* differs from common usage. Hence, ethnic Koreans *(Chōsenjin)* are legally *gaijin* and are treated accordingly. That is, they are denied many civil rights and subject to deportation, even if there is no country to receive them, since the majority were introduced by the Japanese themselves before the governments of North and South Korea were established — a Catch-22 the Japanese have exploited to avoid integration ever since the Allies returned all authority to Japan.

So you anticipated correctly in spirit, since all whites look alike (whether blonde and blue-eyed or not). But the Japanese discriminate against all foreigners unequally.

Why *Eikaiwa?*

Why study English conversation indeed? When only a single-figure percentage of all Japanese people have ever met a foreigner, let alone actually addressed him or her in a foreign language, and when surveys come up with results showing that a clear majority of the population of Japan has no interest in meeting foreigners, you begin to wonder why *eikaiwa* is such big business.

Perhaps big business is the key. Have some wily English conversation school operators bribed the government to keep mouthing slogans about "internationalization" and "cross-cultural communication"? Or are the big men behind the *eikaiwa* boom old schoolfriends or comrades in arms of politicians, so that they don't even need to bribe them to mouth the slogans? Surely not: such corrupt practices could never take place in this country, now could they?

No, the key must be in the consumers (or, as they are politely called, "students") rather than in the operators (polite term: "rip-off sharks"). The students recall their days of studying English for six years or more at school and college, and just can't believe that it was so boring; so they start again, in the often vain hope that it will prove more interesting. Others take it up because the flower-arranging course at their local "culture center" was oversubscribed. Yet others because they think that *eikaiwa* is a totally different thing from *Eigo,* and won't involve things like grammar, pronunciation, words, sentences or anything in books — like the people in English-speaking countries who go to French conversation classes and tell the teacher at the beginning they want to learn only conversational French, so they don't want to study verbs.

It seems there are *eikaiwa* schools that are supposed to be thinly disguised dating agencies, where a course of

"Lessons" can lead to torrid love affairs between infatuated "students" and delighted "teachers." Experience cannot confirm any of this, but nobody can take your dreams away.

In fact, though, really, *eikaiwa* schools are the best place for Japanese people to prove conclusively that *gaijin* really are inferior. Just look at those people who set themselves up as teachers! Young and inexperienced, unwashed and slovenly, exaggeratedly casual and jolly, no self-control when students say something quite reasonable like "Tokyo is *shiti*," can't speak Japanese, and can't even answer simple questions about the rudiments of English grammar. If these are the élite of Western society, chosen to represent it abroad, then God help us all! So drop in at the nearest *eikaiwa* school, or salon as they've started calling them for some unknown reason, and indulge in a spot of comparative culture. You'll soon see how comparatively cultured Japan is.

Why Not English?

Many a foreigner is accosted to the point of persecution by Japanese who want to try out their English. Openers are not "Can I help you?" but "Where do you come from?" Sooner or later, however, most come to learn that in areas where English is essential to business or carrying out responsibility, the vast majority of Japanese actually do not want to learn English.

This is no longer the natural (and healthy) desire to escape compulsory study that has no more relevance than passing exams. Rather, it's the avoidance of the individual responsibility that comes with language ability. Those known to speak English will always be called upon to handle a thankless job fraught with certain error. Worse yet, it may be their lot to go abroad and suffer in alien lands. Certainly poor language skills will ensure the experience is a disaster if not hell. Actual assignments make the Peter Principle look like Peter's Law: the truly competent will be advanced beyond the need for English and the rest doomed like Sisyphus.

The resultant "foreigner complex," simultaneous attraction to and repulsion from foreigners, is an inevitability of the schizophrenic approach to English where the desire to know is killed with the necessity to learn. It begins with the majority of parents who send their children to cram schools to study the very English they themselves avoid like the plague.

In a similar way the Ministry of Education (appropriately

enough on the eve of 1984) announced the official reduction of minimum hours for compulsory English while in the same year spokesmen addressing a conference of high school business and computer teachers asserted that English was essential to future progress and the single top priority for their students.

While it may appear that the left hand doesn't know what the right is doing (bureaucratic schizophrenia is no more unknown in Japan than in the Pentagon or Parliament), many public school English teachers see it as quite consistent with the examination system. The object is not to educate, but to select an élite group. Only those with exceptional ability or exceptional budgets for education can expect to "arrive."

Certainly language skills alone are no passport to the good life. Only the really exceptional simultaneous interpreters, translators and multilingual secretaries can earn more than skilled office workers with no English ability.

The final deathblow to desire comes in the workplace. In most companies, it is deemed pretentious to use English. One more incentive for those with ability to avoid being caught using English in public.

As a result, don't be impatient with people whose opener goes something like "May I speak with you?" And be genuinely appreciative of an honest "Can I help you?" Those who shout "*Harō!*" provide excellent opportunities to practice Japanese.

Why No Understanding?

Why can't people understand English even after six to ten years? There's more to the mystery than the compulsory nature of such a sentence in purgatory. Much of it will be dispelled, however, by a look at the English portion of Examination Hell, which is the gate to Academic Paradise.

Not only is there grammar to perplex any would-be internationalist, but where native English speakers can find several correct possibilities, the Japanese student must guess the only one that will be counted as correct. All others are "wrong" — not the "best choice." In short, only memorized answers will count: those from comprehension (much less comprehensible questions) seldom count. And for many, testing begins even for entry to elementary schools.

What happens at lower levels reveals it is a miracle that any Japanese understands English at all. For example, educational television and radio (NHK) normally teach foreign languages by initially focusing on the sounds of the language and concentrating on the points of greatest difficulty. Russian, Korean, Chinese — all, except English! Even the easy-to-master *th* sounds are neglected for esoteric and less significant distinctions.

Whatever weakness there is in the NHK series looks like strength compared to standard school curricula. Here, students never attempt to master basic consonants but start out memorizing intonation patterns. In private and group study before mandatory junior high English, materials are

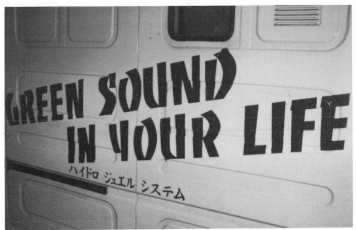

rewritten with Japanese sounds! This actually teaches students that the strange sounds native English speakers are making on tapes can be properly reduced and simplified so that l = r = Japanese ''r'', v = b, th = s or z, and so on. The earlier and longer a student studies, the more there is to unlearn before real English can be understood!

Similarities that actually exist between English and Japanese seem to be deliberately ignored. Because expressiveness is discouraged in formal Japanese, few learn that both English and Japanese intonation function emotively and in the same way. Those who do, have learned the English meaning of individual words. The rest have merely learned to substitute terms and expressions. Thus, ''fine'' never is ''OK'' or ''good'' but equated with ''good spirits'' or ''clear skies'' on a ''case by case'' basis. Further, this approach assumes every English idiom has a Japanese equivalent although there are many Japanese concepts that have no English equivalent — you know, Japanese is richer than English! Only Japanese can understand Japanese!

One experienced English teacher has dubbed this mystifying approach to study ''Unicorn English'' after a highly respected text series used at top Japanese high schools. This series avoids putting adjectives in front of nouns in favor of prepositional phrases, has exercises to change every active voice to passive and equates every English positive expression to Japanese negative and vice versa: English ''Let's'' becomes Japanese ''Why don't we?'' and English ''Why don't we?'' becomes Japanese ''Let's.''

Why Foreigner Japanese?

That is a very good question . . . just why is there a special kind of Japanese for foreigners? Isn't everyday Japanese adequate? Is this some plot to restrict access to the Japanese mind? Some attempt to regulate cross-cultural communication? More of the non-tariff trade barrier system, or merely an attempt to idealize and simplify communication?

Well, yes and no to all of the above. Certainly, intentionally or not, the Japanese language is a barrier to trade. And it would seem that ''Japanese for Foreigners'' is not exactly a smashing of the gate. Since it doesn't provide information about the language in a manner that a good many foreigners would like to see — it walks and talks like a barrier — special Japanese for foreigners perhaps *is* a barrier.

Pity the poor *gaijin* who learn in their Japanese primer

that all verbs end in -*masu,* or -*masen* if they're negative, or -*mashita* if they're past tense. Let them loose on the streets or in the homes of Japan, and nary a -*masu, -masen* or -*mashita* will they hear. Instead of *shimashita* for "did," they may hear just *shita.* But when they scuttle back to their faithful dictionary, to find out the meaning of this mysterious *shita,* all they will find is "tongue" or "down," but not "did." Even the dictionaries are in on the conspiracy to conceal ordinary spoken Japanese from overseas snoopers. And no fair leaving out dirty words and slang like English dictionaries did in ages past!

It certainly looks like a conspiracy when foreigners are only invited observers after all the decisions have been made and challenges to the approach are treated with something less (actually, more) than scorn. Certainly R.A. Miller's attempt to "demythologize" Japanese language studies deserves a more fair reading than slamming it down midway and refusing to read any more as some Japanese scholars have privately boasted. Miller may be guilty of sour grapes and a failure to practice fully what he preaches about documentation, etc., but such reactions on the part of many Japanese suggests he may be closer to the truth than many would like to admit.

It is safe to say that there are some conservative authorities who directly influence the various governmental institutions that regulate affairs of education and language. For them the Japanese language is a rich heritage, unique in all the world. They can't have foreigners fouling it up and showing disrespect, and it might not be patriotic to democratize the language the way the Chinese did on the mainland. No problem with the methods of governmental edict, just don't do away with the myriad social distinctions that confuse innocent *gaijin* and, it must be admitted, not a few citizens of Japan. These distinctions are unlikely to disappear either spontaneously or by government edict, and until they do only *gaijin* will be allowed to address each other as *anata*, calling a *supeido* a *supeido*. For those not willing to enter the vertical society, that's OK, but let's hope for more encouragement for those who do.

So while everyday Japanese is adequate for Japanese, those who respect authority over truth itself will find it inadequate and jarring to find people who express their true thoughts the way foreigners are always trying to do. Nothing less than "the refined Japanese" will do. The refined Japanese *sake*, however, is not everyone's cup of tea.

Why Ask Your Age?

A great mystery is why the supposedly polite Japanese always ask your age. Possibly this is because it's one of the first things Japanese learn and can remember when confronted with a need for small talk in English. All children learn it in the seventh grade if they didn't learn to ask it before English is compulsory. It comes right after *"Imu-fine-sank-you-ando-you."*

At that age every birthday is an event to be remembered, not forgotten. Further, it's a question frequently handled in the vernacular as well, since adolescence is uneven and unpredictable in appearances. (Japanese laws still leave the legal age of consent at thirteen even though they lack uniform sex-education policies to match; most area schools in fact have no such policy.) With age so important at the time English is first studied and English so inessential after college entrance, the later shock of actually using English jolts the memory back to square one and a replay of old Beginners' English tapes: "How old are you?" (pause) "I am fourteen!"

While Andy is talking with Kenji about the New York branch operations, Kenji's wife has been let out of the house to meet the foreigner's wife. She invariably leads a conversation that sounds like a police investigator's search for incriminating evidence.

Lisa doesn't mind "Why did you come to Japan? How long have you. . . ?" etc., but "How old are you?"!!! Keiko-san's voice sounds innocent enough, but Lisa can only respond with her unspoken thoughts:

"She knows, doesn't she. . .? Even with all that makeup she looks twenty . . . but she must be forty if she has teenage children. . . . Why does she have to rub it in like this. . .?" She summons courage, finally:

"Oh, let's see. . . I was born near one of those wars. . . I was awfully little then and it's hard to remember just which one or where it was even. . ."

Of course, Lisa's variation on classical Marx (Groucho, that is) is an appropriate response, but she has missed Keiko's motivation. More than likely she will find that Kenji did the same routine with Andy. In most instances, there is no other way for Japanese to decide if they are junior or senior to foreigners who are outside their social hierarchical categories. Depending on how familiar Lisa wants to be and how much responsibility she wants to assume for herself, a lie toward seniority may be the only improvement on reality here. If Keiko finds Lisa is her junior she may not be so deferential (''polite'') or free with gifts, or follow Lisa's lead.

Perhaps the only, but not necessarily best, way to teach such a host some Western manners is to switch: ''Oh, I've been dying to ask you that question! How old are you?! . . . Oh, I see, and how much salary does your husband make? How much does he give you? Does he keep a second wife?'' — end of conversation!

Why Expensive Restaurants?

There are few visitors to these climes who do not want to get a real taste of the mysterious Orient. Japanese hosts tend to recognize this, but respond to the situation in a strange way when it comes to deciding the kind of restaurant to which they think the unwitting visitor should be introduced.

An inverted sense of inferiority comes into play. Let us imagine the mental discussion that goes on:

''Now, let me see. The visitor will want to try Japanese food, although we all know that foreigners can only stomach a limited range of delicacies — certainly must avoid *natto* and can't be too sure about raw fish or octopus. The place will have to be clean and expensive, and

Chinois café
PICASSO
since 1986

preferably one visited by Jimmy Carter or Prince Charles. Now, if that restaurant tends to be full of foreign businessmen on expense accounts, even better — the visitor will feel at home. On the other hand, perhaps it would be more sensible to play safe and take him to an even more expensive French restaurant — they all love French food and Japanese French food must be the best in the world if we think about how much they charge for it. Yes, that's the thing to do. Look at the advantages: the visitor cannot fail to be satisfied; we can prove how international we are; and it will give us a chance to eat what we normally can't afford, and charge it up to the company!''

The decision is made and the foreign visitor is dragged to a poor pastiche of France complete with sycophantic chefs and superior Noritake sucriers. The only problem is that the visitor may be just a little tired of "international food." And do his Japanese hosts really want him to arrive home with this kind of report:

"Oh, yes, Tokyo was great. The hotel beds were marvelous, I didn't have to tip a soul, and they drove me everywhere in a Cadillac, but I couldn't quite work out why they kept taking me for so-so steaks at phenomenal prices, and as for all that French stuff. . . .''?

The point is, there isn't much about "international food" to write home about. Of course, most visitors would be impressed by their few plates of *shabu-shabu* or Kobe beef, but it still isn't very ethnic food. Now one thing the Japanese do have in abundance is ethnic restaurants — all those *akachochin* squeezed in between dry-cleaning stores and hair salons, with all those wonderful timber beams and bamboo touches ("since 1983"). That's where the visitor should be taken: let them behave as Romans, or rather Tochigians. No visitor should be denied the chance to at least look at a plate of shivering shrimps, pickled locusts or crunchy baby crabs. There he can find the true smells, sights and sounds of the Orient.

Unfortunately, few Japanese businessmen worth their salt realize that there is a certain illogicality to visitors being expected to enthuse over French or Italian cuisine japonaise. There is, instead, the distinct feeling that an *akachochin* might be regarded as primitive, or a trip on the subway embarrassing. Nonsense. The average visitor may well not enjoy being forced to spend hours sitting on *tatami* or playing silly games with geisha, but he will still want to experience something. And in Japan, the more you pay the more uncomfortable and homogenized it can easily become.

Why Raise Umbrellas?

What puzzles many foreigners is why Japanese people always raise their umbrellas when they approach them.

The answer Japanese usually give is that it's because foreigners are so tall. That hardly can satisfy the average foreigner caught in a drizzle.

Indeed, if umbrellas were simply carried normally, *gaijin* could walk through a Japanese crowd during a downpour with the greatest of ease, bumping nary a bumbershoot. But hoisted high, as they all too often are, there is an instant forest of arms and chrome shafts to snag umbrella tendrils whatever way you twist or angle yours to avoid theirs.

Viewed from across the street the phenomenon resembles a hairy caterpillar with sudden indigestion as a lone foreigner wends a way through a stream of Japanese pedestrians. If perchance *gaijin* raise their umbrellas, the worse the case of indigestion witnessed.

Of course, everyone gets less protection the harder the rain and the higher the umbrella, so it hardly can be construed as a gesture of politeness or consideration. Yet, the average Japanese when asked argues precisely so. In an effort to find the real answer, one school of thought

speculates (for speculation is all that is possible) that it is merely mistaken transfer: what would be polite to another Japanese must be ipso facto polite to *gaijin*. That is, in a crowd, raising a few umbrellas to reduce congestion would be polite when everybody is at the same altitude. The fact that at most foreigners' altitude there is no congestion goes unobserved while simultaneously everyone tries to be as polite as possible.

Another more sanguine school accepts the automatic response thesis but insists that motivation is entirely different, i.e., Japanese merely want to speed foreigners on their way mainly to avoid them. This school points to such supporting evidence as that Japanese popularly believe all foreigners stink of butter, garlic, sweat or any combination thereof. (Of course, foreigners "know" the Japanese all reek of fish, garlic and *sake* — both pass each other while holding their breaths and never are wiser from contrary information.) Otherwise Japanese hope to avoid the more odious situation of foreigners stopping to ask questions in English. That their action with umbrellas is self-defeating or working against avoidance is simply due to unthinking automatic, conditioned response to the sight of a *gaijin*.

A third school has yet another explanation that certainly appeals to logic. They insist that while urban Japanese may not appear to be staring at foreigners, the deed is bared by the act of raising their umbrellas. That's the only way they can obtain an unrestricted view.

So, what is to be done? One American advises, "Hunker down and charge — if you can't see them, they can't see you!"

Why Loud Voices?

It's asinine, but it works. For in no other country can you be as sure that if you take ''no'' for an answer, that's just what you get. This Japanese ''no'' should not be confused with the one that really means ''yes.'' This one is expressed very directly with or without apology: *dekinai* (can't be done), *shikataganai* (there's no alternative), *arimasen/nai* (there is/ain't none) or the like. No one *voluntarily* says, ''We found a way after all.''

A third repetition of one of these formulas has the magical power of turning the volume of *gaijin* voices up by several decibels. In turn, loud voices seem to have magical powers of bringing appeasement to their owners (if apoplexy doesn't come first).

Take, for example, the foreigner refused the much cheaper Japanese-style accommodation at a Kyoto inn. Several days for triple-priced Western style was too much for this intrepid traveler who spoke no Japanese. Stage one began at the third refusal, when loud English voices drew a crowd of the curious and a few offers of assistance. At stage two, onlookers began to slink away, then flee. At stage three, after nearly twenty minutes of arm-waving, shrieking and braying, the innkeeper relented. Some observers felt he had grounds to call the police. Others anticipated the need of an ambulance. But respect grew in the hearts of all: some for the tolerance and goodwill displayed by the innkeeper for ten days and for a few others the marvelous effects of loud braying.

In the ranks of the more experienced, too, there may be a confession or two of playing the ass when quick action was desired. Such as when only the price for three of something is displayed but the clerk wants to charge for one of them far in excess of one-third the posted figure, or a bank refuses to honor its own check drawn on another branch. These are good opportunities to practice Japanese: don't wait for a second refusal; just speak loudly and clearly so that all in sight can hear. If you are prepared to repeat yourself a little louder each time, you will find braying really works.

We encourage a less asinine way for more serious transactions and with bureaucracies. Many times, as in our home countries, you get "no" simply because of ignorance — theirs, unfortunately! If time is available, you can educate those you must deal with by being armed with telephone numbers of authoritative sources. Time is needed for them to confirm you are wrong with several intermediaries before yielding to your insistence to call where they can learn you are right.

But far and away the best method plays on Japanese fear of documentation, and the unwillingness to take responsibility on paper for any decision at all. Whether you know Japanese or not, from the first refusal, insist that the given explanation be written out along with time and date and personal seal affixed. Almost invariably a hurried phone call or consultation will precede getting what you want or an adequate explanation of the true state of affairs. In this manner, things that belong in the barnyard can stay there, whatever their origin.

Why *Giri*?

An expression of thanks still common amongst older members of the English-speaking world is "Much obliged!" which is short for "I'm much obliged to you." It suggests a very give-and-take situation, and yet it may not have any real sense of future obligation attached to it. Even so, it is strange that few Japanese seem to know the expression, obligations of all kinds being the very Japanese modus operandi.

The word *giri* is one of those words that has no specific meaning, but a host of shades of meaning, all somehow or other to do with the English word "obligation." It is interesting to look up the word "oblige" in an English dictionary and to be reminded that that also has many uses. The meaning of "to make indebted or grateful to (someone) by doing a favor" is the one being used in the example above, but there is also the meaning of "to bind or constrain (someone to do something) by legal, moral or physical means." And that is the one which the Japanese seem to be stressing when they use the word *giri*.

In cunning hands, this thing *giri* can be imposed on people. The odd useless gift here, the apparent favor there, and the web of obligation is spun by the spider-man who wants the world somehow bound to him. And it is a web in which everyone gets involved, in which everyone finds an unspoken need to repay, or give presents or somehow support those to whom the *giri* is owing. It is insidious and involves large transactions of money.

As one observer of the Japanese scene has commented, just think how much more the Japanese could actually achieve if they didn't spend so much time on all their obligations. On the other hand, a lot of department store business would be lost.

The worrying thing about *giri*, however, is trying to decide what really comes from the heart, and what comes because someone somewhere thinks it should and therefore that you should also be put in a position to do likewise.

It runs through the whole paternal system of business. The boss automatically puts himself into a *giri*-producing situation. He can't ignore it, because it is perhaps the only way he can guarantee true fidelity among his employees, or at least trap them into being unable to leave the company because of all the obligations they have towards him.

The reason everyone encourages this system is that they want the security of knowing that when they are in a time of need the envelopes full of money will definitely flow in, immediately and without question. No need to think·for a moment whether or not you should send money to the funeral; all you have to do is consult the Giri List and decide how much. When the wife of the boss goes into hospital, you will of course have a whip-round in the office to send some flowers, just as you would anywhere else in the world. The *giri* system, however, then demands that she send back individual presents to each person to keep the system going. As these probably cost much more than the original flowers, the boss and his entourage remain ahead in the stakes. How much simpler in the West, for example, when the response would be a simple letter of thanks, just one letter, and that's the end of it.

The number of Japanese who really don't like *giri* much may well be increasing, but it is probably such a part of the whole way the society operates that it can never die out completely.

You scrub my back and I'll scrub yours . . . only I've got a Pierre Cardin sponge.

II
Consumers and Consumption

Why Chopsticks?

The obvious reason is that the Chinese use them, but there's more to it than that. The original chopsticks were one long, supple stick bent in the middle and used like a pair of tongs. It may be that such long, supple sticks were soon in short supply (whether the forerunner of a modern trading company had cornered the market in chop-tongs and forced the price to unaffordable levels and thus unwittingly founded another time-honored Japanese tradition, history does not tell), and people took to using separate sticks in desperation.

There is support for this theory in modern cooking chopsticks, which are still joined at the top with a token thread. Some people say that the thread is so you can hang the sticks on the gas tap, but that is surely an unromantic modern rationalization, which fails to take into account the fact that there were no gas cookers in the Jomon Period. Another theory is that the original chop-tongs kept breaking, and the Japanese people, with an inventiveness and eye for economical avoidance of wastefulness that has become their world-renowned trademark, stopped throwing them away when they broke, and instead continued to use the two separate parts.

Now, the skill of making chop-tongs has disappeared, and even when chopsticks are made joined together, they have to be broken apart before they can be used.

What few people realize is that it is because of chopsticks that Japan is such an economic success. If *salarymen* had

had to use knives and forks for their *bento,* they would not have had one hand free to make phone calls, smoke cigarettes or scratch their, er, feet during lunch — all activities which would otherwise slow their progress during working hours.

Furthermore, it is practice with chopsticks from an early age that makes Japanese people so adept at activities that require strong finger-muscles: *shiatsu* massage, karate, cleaning one's ears on buses and trains, cleaning other people's ears and snipping their nose hairs at barber shops, etc.

Why Disposable Chopsticks?

Hygiene. Next time you go to a restaurant, look around at the other customers and ask yourself how many of them you would be happy to kiss. Find the least kiss-worthy of the clientele, and bearing him or her in mind, come back to the same restaurant the next day; order your favorite dish and, just as you are about to put the first mouthful into your mouth, imagine that the fork you are using was used yesterday by that person. Imagine that the student or Korean employed to wash the cutlery is exhausted and badly paid, and has a grudge against his employers, so that he occasionally slips a fork back into the drawer without washing it. You are using that fork. Now enjoy your meal. You can't? Oh dear, but at least you get some idea of why wooden chopsticks.

It may have been a dream, but it seems there was a column in one of Japan's greatest newspapers saying that a ban on wooden chopsticks for environmental reasons would in fact be environmentally bad, as it would deprive many Japanese people of their last remaining opportunity for direct contact with nature. Those namby-pamby environmentalists who claim that the Japanese have no respect for the world's forests and are quite happy to squander these valuable natural resources for the sake of ostentatious, extravagant consumption should think again, and understand how much less a feeling for nature people would have if they had to use plastic chopsticks instead.

Anyway, the forestry experts assure us that all forests need thinning occasionally, and that the felling of the occasional tree for chopsticks is just good husbandry. Never mind that these "occasional trees" are felled by the square mile: after all, most of them are far enough away in places like Indonesia and Minnesota, so that their effect on the Japanese environment is zero. And think what would happen to the unemployment figures in the chopstick-supplying countries, if a ban were introduced. For how can you retrain a proud chopstick-splitter? These skilled craftsmen of the Southeast Asian islands need years of training to perfect the skill of making a split just the right length, and leaving a join that is not too strong, not too weak, but calculated to give the diner a feeling of achievement at splitting his own chopsticks, without straining himself. Who knows how many thousands of these craftsmen are now alive and putting their skills to a useful end? What a waste it would be not to exploit their abilities!

Back to the washer-up. Don't blame him too deeply for skipping the odd fork. Afer all, if you had to wash up after a Japanese meal with all those tiny little plates, dishes, bowls, chopstick stands and whatever else, you'd be happy to come across wooden chopsticks that you could throw away without washing.

Why *Raisu?*

Why use an English word? Don't they have their own word for it? Well, of course they do. After all, it is the staple diet, and has been ever since, er, well, anyway a long time before English words started to be adopted into Japanese. The problem is actually the opposite: there is not only one word for it, but several: *kome* or *o-kome, gohan, ine, momi* to name but a few. Each of these words stands for rice at a different stage in its existence: seedlings, rice ready for harvesting, uncooked rice, cooked rice, that sort of thing.

When most people in Japan were farmers, they all knew the difference between the words, but now that most live in cities and are so un-countrified that junior high kids can't break an egg or peel an apple (which incidentally would be no problem if they hadn't been sprayed with all kinds of agro-chemical poisons), nobody knows the difference. So to avoid using the wrong one and making a fool of themselves, everybody says *raisu*. Even the dictionaries don't know: one defines *momi* as "husks," another as "rice without its husks," and another as "husked rice," which is clever, as it could mean rice with its husks on or off, depending on how you feel about it.

Nowadays, the only people who think they know the real word for rice in restaurants are *gaijin*, who insist on asking for *gohan*, and then get angry when the waitress replies, *"Ah, raisu desuka?"* What the *gaijin* has done is confuse the waitress even more: as related above, she herself is no longer sure of the real Japanese word, but, being a waitress, she probably has an inkling that at this stage in its existence it used to be called *gohan*. Then, when she hears a *gaijin* say it, she knows the *gaijin* is bound to be wrong, because as everyone knows the Japanese language is very difficult, and this confuses her even more.

Now, why choose the English word? That is a case of cultural intercourse through vocabulary exchange. Because America has been given the characters *bei-koku* or "rice country," the word *raisu* has been accepted in exchange. This may sound like a silly name for America, but in Chinese they use characters that mean "beautiful country," and no Japanese would admit that for any country other than his own.

One more word about *gohan:* nowadays it means "meal" as well as "cooked rice in a bowl." So let's use *raisu;* the last thing we want is confusion, isn't it?

Why Cold *Bentō?*

For one thing, most of the boxes in which *bentō* is served these days are made of flimsy expanded polystyrene. If you put hot food in them, they'd melt and combine with the food, and even in this advanced petrochemical society peo-

ple aren't willing to accept that amount of chemical ad-
ditives in their food. Not yet.

Also, a steaming hot lunch packed by an adoring if
somewhat underslept wife at about 6:50 a.m. into her husband's impressive-looking executive "leather" briefcase
(probably also expanded polystyrene) is bound to lose some
of its heat and freshness by lunch-time, and might steam
up the inside of the briefcase and rust the "stainless" steel
fittings. So why not give up and make it cold, from yesterday's leftover rice? Add a bit of meat from the day before
yesterday's *sukiyaki*, half a sausage that the baby didn't eat
for its dinner, a bit of parsley that was used to garnish a
sushi meal a few days ago, a red pickled plum in the middle of the rice for a patriotic touch, and lo! Your *bentō* is
the envy of your colleagues, who have brought nothing but
a mangy sandwich or a big riceball hastily purchased at the
stall by the station where the hobos spend the night.

After all, if people in the West can enjoy sandwiches,
which are equally cold, why can't people in the East enjoy
cold *bentō*? The purpose is the same, too. Just as the Earl of
Sandwich invented sandwiches so he didn't have to leave
the gambling table for such a trivial matter as his lunch,
now the modern *salaryman* can wolf down his cold *bentō*
while remaining seated at his desk, counter or VDU. And
think of all the time saved by not having to blow it to get it
cool.

But in recent years hot *bentō*, horror of horrors, has
become more and more popular. You can see customers
lining up outside these warm *bentō* outlets, waiting pa-
tiently for an overworked assistant to force rice into the cor-

ners of a square plastic box without breaking the box and splattering the rice all over the counter. What is the country coming to? With all this waiting around to get a hot meal, then more waiting around for it to cool down, well, the next thing will be people demanding a whole hour off for lunch! Is the mushrooming popularity of MacJunk a cause or an effect of this? No, let's stick with cold, chewy rice — better for business, better for productivity, and better for the appetite for a real meal when you get home, or at least on the way home: your dinner is bound to be cold when you get back.

Why One-Inch Toast?

The naming of bread involves a lot of confusion in Japan, bread not being a traditional Japanese staple. The very word used for it, *pan*, is confused. It comes from the Portuguese "pão" and not from the French "pain" as one might assume. More and more these days, however, the packet variety will have an English name on it, such as "English Bread" (not clearly defined) or "Sandwich Pan," which is in fact what any self-respecting British or American housewife would use for toast. No real tradition means total freedom of expression. It also means a lack of understanding of the toast phenomenon. Ask any Japanese under 50 what they have for breakfast at home and the answer will probably be "bread and a cup of milk." This translates into English as "a glass of milk and some toast."

Then there is the extraordinary phenomenon of the real-

ly thick variety which hangs uncomfortably in between the categories of Bread and Toast. It finds particular favor in coffee-shops where it appears as the substructure of ''Pizza Toast'' (another contradiction in terms) or as the stodge element of ''Morning Service'' (which is nothing to do with religion).

This super-bread, generally between one and two inches thick, appears ridiculous to foreigners used to the delicately thin, crispy attractiveness of genuine toast generously overlaid with butter and marmalade, jam or peanut butter. For a start, it is almost impossible to eat, and certainly not elegantly. Watch the poor girls with delicate mouths wondering how to deal with this whopping lump of foreign matter. Moreover, it is rarely served with any kind of confiture and only an iota of margarine, making it roughly the equivalent of *o-nigiri* without the seaweed and the filling. Finally, although it resembles toast on the outside, inside it is still soft and puffy, so how can it be classified?

One suspects that the reasons for its widespread use lie entirely with the perpetrators — the maitres d' of establishments which serve the monstrosity. Surely the customers don't particularly like super-bread? The perpetrators can get away with it simply because most customers are either too busy waking up to complain or too happy gossiping to even notice.

So why do the coffee-shop proprietors serve it up?

1. It is easier to toast two one inch thick slices than four normal slices.
2. You can stand super-bread/toast on its edge to give artistic feeling.
3. They really believe that the hard/soft combination is what toast is all about.
4. It promotes great savings on butter/margarine.
5. Toast is not a delicacy — like rice, it is designed merely to fill the stomach, regardless of lack of flavor.
6. It's fun to watch the girls struggle to get the stuff actually into the mouth and keep the crumbs off their Cardin dresses.
7. In the case of pizza toast, you can pretend it really is a worthwhile snack worthy of a ¥450 price tag.
8. Who wants foreigners in for Morning Service anyway?

Why Strawberry Sandwiches?

A nation that can combine two Western inventions and come up with a toilet-roll music box is well-qualified to put strawberries in sandwiches. And remember, these are not strawberries which have been turned into jam; that would be all right, we suppose. But no, they are fresh strawberries chopped up and mixed in with potato salad, or just by themselves with a soupçon of mayonnaise, or nestling among lettuce leaves and canned tuna-fish.

At least, that's the way it looks in those plastic models in the windows of coffee shops, but we must admit never having had the appetite, courage, sufficient confidence that we wouldn't burst into embarrassing laughter, and all the other things that it would take actually to order one. If you have done so, please let us know about it. If it tastes good, perhaps you don't need to read on.

The eminent Japanologist Don Maloney has already noted the ubiquitousness of cucumber in Japanese-style Western-style food, and there would appear to be a correlation. Red and green are complementary colors, so that a plastic model of a sandwich containing both will be aesthetically very pleasing. What's more, combined with the white of the bread or potato salad, it will reproduce the colors of the Italian flag — ideal if you run a coffee shop called Mirano (sic). Then you can call it an Italian sandwich. Even better, instead of potato salad use macaroni salad, for greater authenticity.

Anyway, what else can you do with strawberries? They're grown in hothouses throughout the year in Japan now, and have lost any reputation they may once have had for being a delicacy. So growers just have to get rid of them as best they can, and it wouldn't be surprising if there was a Strawberry Marketing Board somewhere organizing competitions for new ways of palming strawberries off on a public already sated with greater exotica like kiwi fruit, guavas and papayas. In this way, they're sliced up in salads, used to garnish raw fish, and balanced on top of the caramel pudding on those single-plate children's lunches, only to roll on to the adjacent curry. Whereupon the youngster replaces it and transfers curry sauce to the caramel pudding, which has already slithered into contact with the mayonnaise on the fried prawn, anyway.

When you've been brought up to enjoy dishes like these from such an early, impressionable age, then strawberries in sandwiches will seem like nothing out of the ordinary.

Also, don't forget the nationalism lurking behind the whole thing: people put little red *umeboshi* in the middle of their lunchbox rice to remind them of the national flag. Isn't the appearance of red strawberries in white sandwiches a sinister forerunner of rising nationalism?

Why Noodles?

If the rice-ball *o-nigiri* is to the Japanese child what a cheese-and-tomato sandwich is to an English child, or a hamburger to an American, then surely the Japanese noodle is equivalent to an English cup of tea or a milk shake. It is something essential for recharging the batteries. A bowl of noodles a day helps you work, rest and play.

Take Anchorage Airport as an example. Largely run by clever Japanese-Americans, the place is basically designed to satisfy the motley hordes of Japanese tourists who flock through: beer at ridiculous monopoly prices, expensive

duty-fee brandies, salmon you'd be better off buying in Hokkaido. . . . and SOBA. At any time of arrival or departure there are eager noodle-consumers, particularly businessmen. The interesting question is this: are they on the way back to Japan or on their way out?

If the former is the case, then this could be an indication of pent-up noodle frustration, despite the fact that Soba à la Alaska is about as near Ma's cooking as Ham Sandwich British Rail. If the latter is the case, then it proves that the desire for noodles develops within 10 hours of departing from the Motherland. A market survey should definitely be carried out to determine exactly why several hours on a Jumbo brings on a severe case of sobaphilia or even sobamania.

The usual reason given for the popularity of noodles is their ease of consumption — no fuss, not much mess. This cannot be denied, and it accounts for the financial success of noodle stalls on station platforms. But that is only half the reason. There is something deeper. A bowl of noodles seems to create a sense of oneness, of harmony, maybe even Orientalness: the smell, the steam, the slurp sensation, and nothing much to chew on. The noodle is the ultimate in instant sensory satisfaction.

That is why the Japanese approach a bowl of noodles and the consumption of its contents with such tremendous concentration. It represents five minutes of Paradise. The surroundings are rarely ideal for eating — the middle of Osaka Station, a drive-in full of skiers at midnight, a stand-bar in Ikebukuro with glaring lights, a street-stall in Sapporo in driving sleet — but focus on that soup and life is all right.

Eating noodles without looking is certainly not easy: attention is required in order to finish off the delicacy neatly. Nevertheless, that does not mean that you have to stare constantly down into the bowl as if your life depended on it. But that is what happens. Expect not the joyous pandemonium of Italians at work on a pile of pasta. Noodles do not make for great conversation.

The truth about the *soba* experience is that it is a total one: one hand preoccupied by the bowl, the other by the chopsticks, the eyes, nose and mouth as close to the culinary delights as possible, and the ears joyfully attuned to the surrounding syncopation of slurping.

Why Slurp?

The visiting *gaijin's* first experience of a real, no-holds-barred noodle-slurp à la japonaise comes as quite a shock.

You sit quietly in the corner of a cheap *ramen* restaurant, trying in vain to look inconspicuous and wondering how on earth you're going to move all those scalding hot noodles into your mouth with a pair of splintery wooden chopsticks, when all of a sudden from right next to you erupts a sound like the last dregs of water running out of the bath. You start, look round in a mixture of bewilderment, astonishment and outrage, and see at the next table a neatly dressed gentleman or maybe a petite, be-kimonoed lady, serenely stuffing down great loads of noodles, and slurping away as if his or her life depended upon it.

Why do they do it? Some claim to be unable to eat noodles without making the noise; it's humanly impossible, they say. So then you immediately prove that you are inhuman by doing it silently. Indeed, you also prove that you don't even stand a chance of ever becoming human, as you can't raise the tiniest of slurps, no matter how you try.

Others claim that they do it on purpose, because it makes the noodles taste better. But you find that you spend so much effort on trying to create a genuine slurp that you forget all about the taste.

What it does seem to do, in some way or other, is cool them down sufficiently to go into the mouth in quantities that look bound to scald off the skin of the eater's tongue, palate and esophagus.

The habit (or should we call it a custom, or even tradition?) does seem to be allied with the duty in some other countries to burp loudly after a meal, to express one's appreciation to the host. Surely this is also one of the most important functions of slurping: it sends what modern politicians and journalists call a signal to the staff and customers of the restaurant, which reads, "Here I am eating these delicious noodles, and although they are cheap and may have an unexpected effect on my constipation, I am slurping them as loud as I possibly can to show that I am proud of being a customer here, I am enjoying my meal, and I can recommend others to order the same thing."

Why Not in the Street?

Ice cream tastes much, much better in the street than anywhere else. In the street, you have the added attractions not only of the taste itself, but of the expressions on the faces of passersby: amusement if you get your nose stuck in it and end up looking like a clown; admiration if you catch a molten drip in mid-fall; sympathy if you miss it and it splats on to the floor; glee if it falls on your shoes; rage if it falls on their shoes. Yet in Japan, such street performances are rare. Even the "take-out" ice-cream parlors provide benches for those who don't interpret "take-out" as "take all the way home securely wrapped and insulated with dry ice that you can later put in the toilet for a wonderful dramatic effect."

The same goes for hamburgers, chips (in the British sense of the word), fried chicken and all the other fast foods that have taken Japan by storm recently. About 15 years ago, before the storm hit, some Japanese friends fiercely denied that Japan was next on the list for McColonialism.

We Japanese, they said, don't like fatty foods. We Japanese, they insisted, don't like to eat things with our fingers, and we Japanese don't like to be seen eating in the street. Wrong, wrong, right.

After all, eating in Japan means being surrounded by lots of little dishes — a separate dish for each dish, right down to the last flake of dried bonito or frond of pickled wild bracken. And you can't eat like that in the street. Admittedly, chopsticks require only one hand whereas knife and fork require two, so that you could, theoretically, eat with one hand and wave your commuter pass or hail a taxi with the other, but what about all those little dishes? No, the place for a meal, as every Japanese person knows, is at home on the floor. Therefore, the expression, "The streets are so clean you could eat your dinner off them," just doesn't exist in this country.

There are other good reasons not to eat in the street, and remember that in Japan the streets are so crowded you'd bump into someone the moment you took your eyes off the crowds and sank your teeth into a succulent *ebiburger*. Result: passersby squirted with *sazan island* dressing, and your own face smeared with reconstituted *ebi*, ketchup, limp lettuce and maybe even a strawberry.

Why Bananas?

"Why are bananas cheaper than tomatoes?" asks innocent little Virginia. "Elementary, my dear Virginia," as Sherlock might say, "just a question of supply and demand.''

"Yes," Wato-san might chime in, "since after the war when bananas were so expensive, the Japanese government has a policy to assure a good supply."

"Well, then, what about beef, oranges and coffee? . . . and the fact I can grow tomatoes on my window sill for free — especially those little cherry ones that rival the price of beef?" (A petulant Virginia, this one.)

"Hmmm, come to think of it, there must be more here than meets the eye. It needs looking into."

Obviously our Sherlock is not Mr. Holmes. Bananas were practically unknown in his day and banana republics were just aborning with the aid of the U.S. Marines to "protect American investments," as in Nicaragua from 1912 to 1933. (This is in any family encyclopedia, but not in U.S. history books. Japan is not the only country with a textbook problem.)

After taking Guadalcanal, the U.S. Marines helped Japan, too, since Japan cannot have "peace-keeping forces" abroad where bananas grow.

"A harmonious process that is," our intrepid Sherlock might continue. "A simple tie-up on the business side and the marines can protect the investments of both countries in places like the Philippines or Taiwan. Of course, since the Americans can't pay bribes, up to 15 percent off the top must come from the Japanese side. This ensures the happiness of the local authorities who must provide adequate 'incentive' for the otherwise ignorant and lazy types who can't appreciate substandard wages and above-standard quotas."

While our Sherlock may be talking through both sides of his deerstalker, a real-life one names names and gives figures (all in Japanese, to date) in a 1985 book entitled *Banana to Nihonjin* (Bananas and the Japanese).

Of course, if we think about it, it's pretty obvious that banana pickers do not get paid enough to send even one of their kids to college (so they have more kids to pick bananas — right?). But Japan's tomato pickers work literally within a stone's throw of most commuter trains, so it would be hard to say their kids don't deserve to go to cram school and college if they want to give it a try — at any rate the possibility is less remote for Japanese tomato pickers.

Just as the government assures a good supply of bananas, it assures the tomato pickers get their income, profit and bananas guaranteed before any challenge to the system gets competitive. One produce-pricing scandal involved undermining the fixed price established by bids on sample lots — fixing the prices seemed scandalous only to foreigners.

Further, as if to keep pace with bananas which are shipped rock-hard green in air-conditioned holds (if so much as one banana in a container is yellow, the whole container is sent back), tomatoes are similarly not allowed to ripen for ordinary retail. Vine-ripened tomato prices boggle the mind almost as do the prices for melons that aren't vine-ripened — but that is another story. As for those cherry tomatoes, Virginia, that's easy: they're vine-ripened and laboriously hard to pick.

Why Buy *Shōchū?*

Why are Japanese beer, wine and liquor prices so out of line? Or, rather, why do they fall in line virtually everywhere? Price-fixing! Along with gullibility and greed unofficially reinforced by the official tax structure. Except for imports and small local manufacturers of *sake,* Japanese alcoholic output is controlled by the wholesalers who deliver to retailers. If any retailers should get out of line, they can count on difficulties with future deliveries.

Exceptions to universal pricing of Japanese beer are so rare that they become national news stories. Restaurants or bars are free to price upwards, but downward pricing resorts to subterfuges such as purchase coupons (1-10 percent) that can be used for future purchases in kind or gift certificates sold at a discount after first being used for a tax dodge. Unless you are placing a very large order the possible savings are as much trouble to find as the out-of-the-way discount shop.

Taxes are applied in a complex fashion based on volume, beverage type and/or intended retail price. Each category ends up with a different rate system, while Okinawa is altogether separately taxed. Beer is confusing by the fact it is taxed at a flat rate by volume (independent of alcohol content) but sold at different prices depending on the container used. The cheapest price (633 ml bottles) therefore has the highest percent tax represented in its price. Smaller or novelty units have less of their price for tax and more for the container, to make the same beer more expensive in the end.

Luxury whiskeys, brandies, etc. are taxed as a percentage of retail price (50 percent or so) but by volume at cheaper prices so that most such labels could be as profitable sold at "discount." This is seldom done since that market is based solely on price, not quality or taste.

The height of gullibility, however, is realized in the *sake* market, for here people should be expected to know better. Of course, the government isn't going to discourage voluntary taxes and distributors are cozy with things as they are. The result is that only a few connoisseurs and those who read the tax law understand that the principal difference in second, first and special grades of *sake* is purely the tax rate: second grade tax is a little over ¥400 per 1.8 liter unit; first grade double that, special grade, triple. Hence the well-known but poorly understood fact that the best *sake* is always second grade (but second grade is by no means always the best!).

Domestic wines are simply more expensive to produce so that imports which are taxed at low rates are the best for your yen as long as you don't do what the stores hope you will do: pay a premium for old white and new red!

Stingy bargain-hunting guzzlers, however, will do best to follow Japanese examples and buy *shōchū*. These distilled spirits of varying potability offer the lowest price (and tax rate) per gram actual alcohol and the best chance to combat greedy price-fixers and escape the ranks of the gullible. *Shōchū* has been fashionable recently, too.

They say all this is going to be "simplified" in the name of trade friction, but we all know what that means.

Why the Kick in *Sake?*

With alcoholic content ranging from 12 to 21 percent, many a Japanologist has wondered about this one — and at least one in print. Could it be the mythical brew has been confused with *shōchū* (any number of distillates from various sources that range from 25 percent upward)? After all, both resemble water and could be easily confused by the uninitiated who have little appreciation for the taste of either.

This is a possibility we won't dismiss out of hand. But we're inclined to believe most imbibers have the more mild-mannered brew in mind. For, like any mule, it kicks from behind — and how!! Few overindulgers remember how much they drank before their suffering, but most remember what gave them a kick in the head when they were down.

Sake has the greatest potential to do this, especially if you have a beer or two beforehand to "open up the pores in your stomach." All naturally produced alcoholic beverages rely on yeast to change sugars and enzyme-modified starches to ethyl alcohol. At the same time, however, yeast produces varying amounts of other substances that are considerably more toxic. They are the usual causes for pain the morning after. Amyl alcohol (fusel oil) is a particularly familiar culprit found in smooth but cheap whiskeys (as a result of distilling off too large a fraction).

Japanese *shōchū*, however, is neither noted for smoothness nor amyl alcohol. While certain varieties may taste like spoiled tequila (of course, tequila tastes like spoiled *Satsuma imo* — sweet potato — *shōchū*), most are well-reputed to be the safest Japanese product from the perspective of morning-after effects.

Sake, however, relies on its enzymes coming from a symbiotic combination of yeast with a fungus (known together as rice *kōji*) to allow conversion of starches to alcohol. To our knowledge, no one has done comparative studies to objectively determine precisely how much after-kick is produced, but foreigners and Japanese concur in describing *sake* hangovers as their worst.

We know of one whose initiation with *taruzake* (*sake* drunk cold from cedar kegs) has led to an insistence that once in a lifetime is enough for overindulgence with *sake*. We conclude from the description of feeling about to die but being afraid of not doing so, that never is better.

III
Communication and Confusion

Why Three Styles of Writing?

Certainly this has nothing to do with the Japanese innate sense of beauty and simplicity, for a text written in the normal mixture of *kanji*, *hiragana*, and *katakana* can hardly be called aesthetically pleasing. The eccentric squiggles of *hiragana* match neither the intricacy of *kanji* nor the angularity of *katakana*; a sentence in which all the real meaning is concentrated in a couple of cryptic *kanji*, but looks miles longer because of a long string of almost meaningless grammatical endings in *hiragana*, is neither visually nor semantically symmetrical. And is it fair to Japan itself that *Nihon* can be polished off in two insignificantly simple *kanji*, while most other foreign nations take up half a line of *katakana* clumsily attempting to represent the original pronunciation or spelling? A Japanese text liberally sprinkled with *katakana* words is one of the ugliest (and even to Japanese people most difficult to read) sights in the history of printing.

So why use 'em? The reason is that first of all *kanji* are necessary because they are one of the very first examples of Japanese cultural borrowing from overseas, and symbolize the deep debt of gratitude which is owed to Chinese culture for its civilizing influence on the Yamato people so many centuries ago.

As for the two *kana* syllabaries, they are pure Japanese inventions which symbolize the Japanese skill of borrowing overseas technology and improving on it. When *kanji* came over, it was soon realized that they were OK for Chinese,

湖上での注意
ウインドサーフィン等の水難
事故が多発しております。
必ず救命胴衣を着用して下さい。
山中湖村・富士吉田警察署
Notice
Don't forget take your Lifejacket to play
Windsurfing for it's yourself

with its lack of grammatical inflections, but not so good for Japanese, which has them. And so, a mere 400 years or so after *kanji* first came to Japan, a brilliant prince, poet, philosopher, sage, demi-god "invented" *kana,* by simplifying certain *kanji* and assigning them their original pronunciation without their original meaning. This act of sheer brilliance has been hailed far and wide, and it is only sullen troublemakers who try to point out that it is a far from original idea, as even ancient Chinese characters contain pronunciation elements, and the development of the European alphabets well over 1,000 years earlier is also one of progress from pictograms to representation of pronunciation.

Newly arrived foreign residents in Japan are advised to learn *katakana* first, so that they can read menus in Western-style restaurants. Japanese elementary school first-graders, on the other hand, are forced to learn the more difficult *hiragana* first, so that they are not exposed at that tender age to all the nasty foreign words that are normally put in *katakana.*

Why Top to Bottom?

Well, why not? It must be better than reading diagonally, or spirally, in random directions, as the Greeks and Babylonians used to. And if you think about it, writing horizontally is not so good for things like inscriptions on banners, titles on the spines of books, graffiti on lamp-posts, danger warnings on telegraph poles.

So, vertical is good, and as for top to bottom and not bottom to top, well, the top seems the obvious place to start, except in the case of road markings, when the writing often runs from the bottom, for reasons that are obvious to the speeding motorist but were not taken into consideration by ancient Chinese sages.

But why right to left? Well, this one is a bit more difficult, especially when you consider that each individual *kanji* is written from top to bottom and from left to right, for an obvious reason adequately explained later. Perhaps it's got something to do with the way scrolls were rolled and unrolled but then we would have to ask why scrolls were rolled and unrolled in that direction rather than the other. And we'd be back where we started.

No, the reason is in fact much simpler: it's always been like that — a reason that a nation with such a lengthy history as Japan can often state with pride. Indeed, until very recently Japanese was written and read from right to left even when it was horizontal, and was only forced to start at the left by the U.S. Occupation in one of those educational reforms that politicians now claim sapped the

lifeblood of the youth of Japan much more than any pre-war fascism, secret policing and forced conscription could ever do. You still see right-to-left horizontal writing on commercial vehicles, on account of the feeling that the words should start at the front of the vehicle. It sometimes happens to English words, too; so don't despair for the Japanese command of English if you see a big truck bearing the slogan YREVILED TPMORP, YDEEPS. But phone numbers are always left to right. If you see SEMIT NAPAJ — 03-453-5311, don't dial 1135-354-30 to complain.

Or perhaps the reason for reading top to bottom is to be found in modern plastic surgery. Nowadays, people can pay a surgeon to make their eyes look "rounder" and "more Western," and for some inscrutable reason many still do part with their money for this purpose. But plastic surgery is new; the only way the ancients had of making their eyes look rounder was by reading up and down, up and down.

Why Left to Right?

Here, *kanji* means each single *kanji,* not whole sentences of them. Whole sentences can be written from top to bottom, right to left, or horizontally in either direction, depending on historical date, purpose, personal taste and the side of the truck you happen to be painting. But the order of strokes in writing each individual *kanji* character is always left to right, top to bottom. There are very, very few strokes that can be written right to left, and they are mostly diagonals or curves, and so don't count.

Here's why. Take a calligraphy brush in your right hand. If you are left-handed, then go back to the cradle and be rigorously, not to say viciously, trained away from that terrible, unforgivable aberration, and then, like everybody else, take a calligraphy brush in your right hand. Put on a kimono with long, flowing sleeves. If you don't want to dirty the kimono with the brush you are holding, put the brush down for a while and serve you right for not reading all the instructions over in advance. Next dip the brush in a generous amount of thick, black ink, and write a big *kanji* on a piece of paper. Any *kanji* will do, but the more complex it is, the better our purpose will be served. For you should try to write the *kanji* you have chosen not from left to right, as is conventional, but from right to left.

Then you will see that you will trail the sleeve of your kimono in the fresh ink, thus spoiling either a fine article of clothing or a fine specimen of calligraphy, depending which branch of ancient Japanese culture is your bag, or both, if you just like everything about this wonderful country. No cheating by rolling the sleeves up or, if you are a married woman, wearing *tomesode* cutback sleeves.

Now change your kimono, pick up your brush again, and write another *kanji,* this time obeying the left-to-right rule. Lo! No mess! Or at least no mess on account of the kimono sleeve.

But, but, but, you cry, *kanji* are originally Chinese, and the Chinese don't wear kimono. Well, maybe not, but they did wear clothes with long sleeves. QED.

But, but, but, but, but, you continue to protest. Weren't the earliest *kanji* carved on tortoise shells and bovine scapulae, the obvious materials for writing on if you haven't invented paper yet? And sleeves don't smudge bone carvings, do they?

Shut up. You know too much.

Why *Gairaigo?*

Gairaigo — words imported into Japanese from other languages, mostly English — exist in such proliferation that there are even special dictionaries for them, hefty tomes that need revising and expanding even before they hit the shelves. French speakers may complain about franglais, but the foreign words in Japanese beat them hollow, and seem to cause little — er, 'ow you say in English? — chagrin. Why do the Japanese adopt into their language so many, many words from a distant foreign language that they themselves admit, nay insist that they cannot speak?

One thing is for appearance's sake. If you use a few foreign words, it gives the impression that you can speak a foreign language, and marks you out as something approaching a genius. Never mind if you've really no idea what you're talking about: you can be sure that no one will have the gall to challenge you. It's like the emperor's new clothes. Research has shown that *gairaigo* expressions are used on those electrical appliances where you don't even need to read the instructions to operate them: in other words, the impressive *gairaigo* are only for show.

As a result, *gairaigo* are like chameleons: they take on the meaning of the moment (much like words like "freedom" or "democracy" in almost any language). Then, sometimes, they get stuck in a particular meaning, and stay there. Often it's a meaning that does not exist in the language of origin. A simple example that springs to mind is *sābisu,* from the English word "service." Now in Japanese it means something like "free gift," hardly one of its most frequent usages in English. On the other hand, try to use the word with one of its native meanings, like, "Please service my car," and all you'll get is blank stares.

This naturally points to the theory that the *gairaigo* in Japanese may not actually be there to confuse Japanese speakers, but to stymie English speakers struggling to learn Japanese. The way it's done is a neat subterfuge: first lull the unwitting *gaijin* into the false sense of security of the feeling that Japanese is just English written in *katakana,* then sweep the rug from under his feet. He will find out that "situation," "condition," "rule" are all OK, and by

natural extension he will assume that "circumstance," "state," "regulation" will also be readily understood if he carefully Japanizes them: *saakansutansu, suteito, regyureishon.* More blank stares. Collapse of learner's confidence. Next victim, please.

Note to serious learners: the three words above may, of course, soon be in the *gairaigo* dictionaries. After all, there are not many new ones left to choose from.

Why *Kōhī* and *Tabako?*

Why are *kōhī* and *tabako* Japanese words? Actually any word rendered into Japanese characters takes on Japanese characteristics. Linguists would have to call even names so rendered "Japanese," just as we think of the different forms for John (from Juan to Jan or Ion) as the same name in different languages (Spanish, Polish or Rumanian). Japanese for John is *Jon,* but pronounced very differently from what American readers might expect — more like the British "John" than the American, which to Japanese ears sounds like "Jahn." When used as a name for a Japanese person (or more often a dog) it ceases to be English or any other foreign language, and becomes Japanese.

On the other hand, a less scientific approach is often to be observed: words derived from a Western language into Japanese are popularly thought to *be* English rather than *from* English — even if actually from French, German, etc.

This superficial approach is reinforced by the way the writing system is used. When Chinese characters are used it is automatically assumed the word is of native Japanese or Chinese origin. Many dictionaries even distinguish the origins by using the flowing *hiragana* for native origins and the angular *katakana* for Chinese. As any Chinese can tell you, however, all are Japanese, not Chinese, in everything but form. This includes meanings and nuance, as well as pronunciation.

Thus, for centuries, coffee was "Japanese," using two Chinese characters invented to reflect the original Portuguese. Then when the number of characters were reduced in the required curriculum, coffee became "English," actually Dutch in origin, by using *katakana* for *kōhī.* Now it languishes in Sino-Anglo-Porto-Hollo-Japanese limbo, since the Chinese characters are still used in signs and advertising.

Another fate befell tobacco. When its characters fell from common use, hiragana *tabako*, meaning "cigarettes,'' became standard. Nevertheless, many dictionaries use *katakana*, while most Japanese are surprised to learn English uses the term for all forms of the weed, not to mean just ''cigarettes.''

Quite similar mix-ups have occurred with a great variety of words that entered Japanese before modernization in the 1860s. Most of these words are from Portuguese and Dutch. The kicker comes in the last decade, however, when Ministry revisions changed many native zoological and botanical terms from Chinese characters to *katakana*. The excuses for this are that the original *kanji* are too difficult for modern superkids, and they couldn't be written in *hiragana,* because the way Japanese is written without spaces between the words would make them difficult to recognize. Now, ''English'' is becoming enriched in many younger minds since everyone knows all ''foreign'' words are written in *katakana;* therefore all *katakana* words were originally English!

How's that for double Dutch?

Why Is "No" "Yes"?

This is not a case of ''The lady doth protest too much,'' to misapply Hamlet out of context. It's a lot more like ''Yes, we got no bananas,'' but not exactly. In fact, most explanations fail to explain it well enough to eliminate confusion, since part of the answer is cultural and a large part is due to the different ways the Japanese and English languages work.

Culturally, as has been noted or can easily be inferred from other observations in this book, the Japanese are conditioned to do what is expected or to give the answer they think is expected. Miscalculation on this point alone covers a good third of the surprising answers you may get when Japanese attempt English "communication." It is hard for Japanese to grasp that you really want to know how — or if — they like coffee, are hungry, tired or what have you.

More understandable — if less forgivable — is the put-off kind of "yes" simply used to delay the moment of reckoning with the fact that the answer is actually "no" — a don't/ a can't/ or a why-don't-you-understand no.

"Ah, these perfidious Japanese," you could find yourself thinking in despair or heartfelt malice, depending on how much the misunderstanding cost you. "This fabled reluctance to say 'no' makes white, black or outright bloody red-dripping lies more acceptable — to them!"

In fact, however, the frequency of this kind of "no" by saying "yes" is perhaps no greater than in most cultures. They are usually well-branded with wishful thinking, vague time schedules, baleful eyes, nervous twitches and/or the like. Indeed, these put-off answers probably comprise no more than five percent.

This leaves a good 60 percent that can be blamed on the mismatch of conceptualization between English and Japanese. Most Japanese learn to think *hai* and *iie* are literally equivalent to English "yes" and "no." At the same time few English speakers learn the literal thinking pattern of Japanese with the inevitable result that neither the English nor the Japanese native speaker is equipped to correct or confirm the other's intention.

Such was most certainly the case when U.S. President Reagan thought Japan's Prime Minister Nakasone had agreed in principle to U.S. raids on Libya — Nakasone had in fact not agreed.

Why Is "Yes" "No"?

Under ideal conditions, at least Biblically, English "yes" is "aye," and "no" is "nay." "No" is basically an adjective, so that in its use as a one-word answer it usually applies to the subject or other nouns. Hence the requirement to add "not" in the predicate of negating sentences: "No, it is not so." "Yes" is an adverb, and so there is no need for additional confirmation: "Yes, it is so."

So English, as this simple explanation shows, is clear, rational, logical, sane and easy. Japanese, however, really does not function in a subject-predicate relationship (thus putting a crimp in generative grammar theory). A Japanese statement works more like the name of the situation for the speaker (thus creating the usefulness of honorific language: people don't give and take — there are bestowals, offerings-up, transfers and receptions, depending on the speaker's relation to the action). The application of "yes" (*hai* or *ee*) and "no" (*iie* or *iya*) corresponds to the appropriateness of such naming of the situation. Japanese *hai* is better thought of as "That registers" while *iie* is more on the order of "That's false." The following typical exchange illustrates just how easily these slight differences can really cross up lines of communication:

RON: How's it going, Yasu?

YASU: Yes, pretty good. . .

RON: Say, didn't you try to call me last night?

YASU: Yes.

RON: Well, what did you want?

YASU: Nothing.

RON: But you did call, didn't you?

YASU: No, I didn't.

RON: I thought you just said you called last night!

YASU: No, I never said such a thing!

Since Yasu had learned to equate everything in English to something in Japanese (just as most foreigners learn to equate Japanese to English with equally frustrating results), he actually thought something like the following:

RON: How is your health, Yasu?

YASU: I heard your question. My health is very good. . .

RON: By the way, the situation is that you didn't try to call me last night or. . .?

YASU: Yes, (that registers — correctly).

RON: Uh, is there something wanted by you?

YASU: There is nothing. . .

RON: However, there was a call by you, wasn't there?

YASU: That's false, there wasn't (a call by me).

RON: It was thought by me that last night there was a call by you was exactly said by you!

YASU: That's false. There never was such a thing said by me!

The only solution is to reconfirm what you think the result of yes or no must mean by restating it in your own words and demanding the same in return.

And if that isn't enough, remember that the colloquial Japanese corruption of *iie* and the colloquial English corruption of "yes" both end up sounding the same: *ya*!

Why Jackets With Slogans?

This is a wonderful example of the Japanese ability to take over a Western fashion (in this case the unpleasantly garish U.S. baseball jacket), and turn it into an expression of the contemporary Japanese spirit in all its ramifications.

Ramification One is simply that aspect of the Japanese spirit that makes it latch on blindly to any fashion foisted upon it by the U.S., whether it makes sense to the Japanese style of life or not.

Number Two is that characteristic of the Japanese which is so often mentioned by anybody from enthusiastic cultural anthropologists to disgruntled Western industrialists teetering on the brink of bankruptcy because of fierce Japanese competition. Conformism. Group identity. So, if you join a tennis club, what better way to proclaim your conformity with all the other members than by wearing their jacket? Don't worry if its slogan is a miraculous concoction of puerile nonsense expressed in badly spelt, anti-grammatical English complete with the occasional unconscious obscenity. What matters is that you all wear the same puerilities, the identical grammatical howlers. *Let's*

Tenis! Its the spilit of yuth and balls. Since 1986.

Number Three contradicts Number Two. Surely anyone who has the audacity to walk round in public with *Young Woman's Univer City Having Good Time Nice Day Just You and Me. No. 7, Yamada Kaori* is hardly trying to melt into the crowd. Isn't this more like a fierce announcement of individuality? Personal rather than group identity? It must take considerable personal courage to wear these gruesome items of apparel and know that every *gaijin* in the street is secretly, or maybe not so secretly, laughing himself or herself blue in the face at such a ridiculous display.

Another interesting suggestion has been made that these jackets are the best way to cheat in exams, now that computerized watches with built-in dictionaries, writing on shirt cuffs, and bribing the examiners have all been banned. The idea is that the words on your back may help your friend sitting behind you. But the fact is that it's a bit more insidious than that. Far from being calculated to help a friend, the words are actually cunningly full of mistakes, so that the ''friend'' is cheated, and the one who gains the advantage is the one who cannot see the back of his own jacket, in other words the candidate himself. If universities get round to banning these jackets from exams, what other methods of cheating will be invented?

Why Baseball *Rōmaji*?

Now, if we admit that Japanese baseball is as different from the genuine American thing as *curry rice* is from vindaloo, then we can only expect contradictory practices in the way it is carried on here. Some things have resisted the Japanese passion for adaptation: the same style of pajamas for players and managers alike, the same balls and bats, roughly the same rules. But one aspect has strangely resisted change, and that is the way players have their name embroidered on their uniforms — always in *romaji*.

This state of affairs begins to show itself at high school baseball level. The players still only have numbers at that stage, but some schools choose to use *romaji* while others stick, quite rightly, to *kanji*. However, once we go profes-

sional, there's not a *kanji* uniform in sight. The *kanji* names remain on the scoreboard, of course, presumably for the reason that they take up less space. But why not *kanji* uniforms?

In some instances the reason could be the use of the same sound but different *kanji*. Superstar Oh chose to use an 'h' in his name, so one enterprising player whose name would normally be written OHARA instead decided to combine Oh and current star Hara to produce OHHARA, which looks silly and impossible to pronounce to us, but no doubt satisfies him — and as it's on his back he doesn't have to look at it anyway.

Let's look at the other possible reasons:

1.   It's a way of pretending that we really believe baseball is international.

2.   Some spectators can't read the *kanji* on the scoreboard, so we'll give them another chance if they can't recognize the player, don't remember his number or can't hear the announcement.

3.   The embroiderers are afraid to make a mistake with *kanji*. If they make one with *romaji*, nobody cares.

4.   It looks better in photographs, rather in the way that foreigners who can't read *katakana* think lanterns bearing the words "ASAHI BEER" look really artistic.

5.   *Kanji* are more difficult to read from a distance and it would be embarrassing to make a mistake with the reading and shout out "*Kattobase*, Rakugō!" instead of "*Kattobase*, Ochiai!"

6.   We have to save foreign players any further embarrassment by allowing them to know who they are playing

against. The only problem with them is that they have names too difficult to pronounce, so we call them "GARY" instead of RAJSICH (and pronounce it "*gēri*" to sound like the word for diarrhea) or "ANIMAL" instead of LESLEY because it's more fun. But on their salaries who's arguing anyway?

Why *Nengō?*

A regular system of dating based on some fixed event in the past, such as the AD/BC system or the Islamic system, is so obviously convenient for gaining an objective historical perspective on events of the last two millennia or so — the years of recorded history. Japan, however, sticks to the old Japanese, sorry Chinese, tradition of renaming eras every time a new emperor comes along. Japanese history is taught using these era names, while the Japanese version of world history uses the AD/BC dates, with the result that nobody can be sure whether World War I was in the Meiji Era (no — it was Taisho) or if the An'ei Era fell in the 18th century (yes — 1772-1780). And so on.

And it gets worse. Until the Meiji Era (1868-1912), eras sometimes had their names changed in mid-reign, for propitious reasons, much as sumo wrestlers nowadays suddenly change their names, and JNR became JR.

What's more, the An'ei Era, for example, was in that vague thing called the Edo Period — the 250+ years when Tokyo was Edo and Edo was capital, or rather not capital. Or should we say "An'ei Period" and "Edo Era"? Nobody is really sure. What about Meiji? Was that a Period or an Era? It's one *nengo,* to be sure, but it covered 45 years, while the previous 45 years had seen all of ten different ones! And Meiji represents a cultural context, attitude, environment, just as much as the term Edo did. So perhaps it should be called a Period, or was it an Era?

This is all very confusing. Era, Period, Period, Era — let's look at the Japanese words for them and fix a separate translation, signed and sealed by all the best translators and authorities, and earn the gratitude of our grandchildren — indeed, start a new era of clarity and understanding. What is the Japanese for Edo whatever-it-is? *Edo-jidai.* OK, so let's fix for posterity the English translation of *jidai;* then there can be no confusion with the other one. What is the other one? What is the Japanese for An'ei . . . on second thought, An'ei wasn't so important, so let's take another . . . er . . . I know, the *nengo* when the *Edo-jidai* began . . . eighth year of Keicho, wasn't it? So what is the Japanese for Keicho era-period-or-whatever? It is, wait for it, *Keicho-jidai.* It's the same! So it's only the English that's confusing!!

In Japanese it's crystal-clear: call them all *jidai,* long or short, propitious or ominous, emperor-related or not, and historical perspective be damned. So now we can say with perfect comprehensibility that the *Edo-jidai* began in the eighth year of the *Keicho-jidai;* the *Keicho-jidai* kept going for a dozen or so years, and then was succeeded by a few dozen other *jidais* in turn, including the *An'ei-jidai* mentioned above, and ending up with the *Keio-jidai,* which was the last *jidai* of the *Edo-jidai,* which is sometimes also called the *Tokugawa-jidai.* A veritable *jidai-matsuri!*

The Japanese have been understandably quite satisfied with this easy-to-follow system for centuries, and there is no reason at all why they should want to change it. Indeed, the government wanted to make it official a few years ago. But if it's survived for centuries, or rather for so many *jidai,* without even being official, who needs government recognition?

IV
Apparel and Appearance

Why Few Kimono?

You rarely see anybody wearing a kimono these days. Like everything else, except perhaps the weather, this is the government's fault. Not the present government, but the Meiji government in 18-something-or-other. In that year a decree was proclaimed, or a proclamation was decreed if you prefer, that Western clothes should be worn for official business. Immediately every rascal and vagabond in Tokyo adopted Western dress, so that it would look as if he was on official business.

The suit soon became so entrenched in Japanese life and culture that the word for a suit, *sebiro* (originally from London's Savile Row) was actually given *kanji* characters, and rather appropriate ones at that, for they mean "back broad," and indeed a man in a suit does appear to have a broader back than one in kimono — unless he plays or sings in a Kabuki or Bunraku theater, when he will wear wings on his shoulders of such dimensions as have no Western parallel.

Women now wear traditional dress more often than men, but even so, not very often. One reason is the price. Check the prices one day in a department store, or one of those kimono shops where an assistant is constantly prowling around at the entrance like a spider at his web. You will soon see how much it is to the advantage of this human spider to catch just one fly in the shape of a customer a month: it will pay for his salary that month, with plenty left over for the shop.

But it's not only price. Everyone knows that the Japanese make it a hobby of theirs to spend as much money as possible on items that are as expensive as possible. So why don't they buy kimonos? The answer is that they do! A girl can expect a seven-figure kimono when she's 20, but then wear it once before she consigns it to her bottom drawer, where it will languish forever. Because after she gets married, she won't be able to wear that style any more, because of the long sleeves that signify an unmarried woman. The old custom used to be for a married woman to cut off the sleeves of her unmarried kimonos and keep on wearing them, incidentally using the sleeves to make baby clothes. But can you imagine anyone in modern, prosperous Nippon doing that?

The real reason is fires and earthquakes, tall buildings and panties. In the early years of Showa, tallish office and department stores appeared in Tokyo for the first time. There was once a fire at a store, but shop girls on the upper floors, who were wearing kimono, refused to jump to safety because they had dressed according to custom with no panties. Thus if they jumped they might expose themselves to the firemen and bystanders below, and so they chose to die a chaste death rather than live a life of shame. Now, women who need to go anywhere above the first floor of a building (and who doesn't?) wear Western dress, with Western underwear, just in case disaster strikes and they have to jump.

Why Panties in Bed?

This curious sociological aberration of the Japanese female seems to be the result of various factors — mythological, historical and practical. But whatever the reasons, it has become an economic incentive to maintain the status quo. One has to respect the Japan Inc. Lingerie Manufacturers' deception that can persuade a gullible market not only that a woman is naked without bras, slips, girdles, pantyhose and the like, but also that two pairs of panties are the minimum requirement over a 24-hour period.

The official rationale is that it is cleaner, nicer on the sheets, warmer and safer to put on clean panties after one's bath and before jumping into one's bed. Nothing is said about it being more uncomfortable. Under close questioning individual women came up with an assortment of reasons as to why they went along with this strange practice.

1. It is all to do with grandmothers telling their grandchildren about the need to cover up their navels to keep the hungry Thunder God off. The argument ignores the fact that most modern panties do not cover the navel or would be likely to deter the god anyway. It still holds up as a good argument for men wearing *haramaki*, however. This is the mumbo-jumbo mythological argument.

2. There have been incidents in this disaster-prone land of women refusing to be rescued from a great height at

night because they did not wish to reveal their secrets to the gaping crowd of well-wishers below. Understandable, but this argument applies to any country, and the disaster could just as easily strike when you're in the shower. Unconvincing.

3. It's cleaner. Again, this may be true, but other nationalities don't see the problem. What's more, two pairs a day increases the laundry bill or laundry effort. Dubious.

4. It feels nicer. How can constricting underwear feel nicer? Perhaps they mean more secure, which is understandable. But basically a non-argument.

5. Men like it that way. This is a bizarre argument. Most women who say this actually only wear panties in bed when there isn't a man with them! Do men really think that? Women wearing panties out of bed can be attractive, but not particularly in bed — well, not for long, anyway.

6. It's a habit.

Yes, it's a habit, but not necessarily historical. Although not many women will admit it, particularly to foreigners, the kimono is best without panties. One reason is that Western-style underwear leads to unsightly lumps in the line of the kimono. Another is that trying to use a Japanese-style toilet wearing a kimono and panties is almost as bad as trying to use any toilet wearing a one-piece ski-suit. The proof of the kimono situation is easily had at gatherings such as the *Bon Odori*, when older women can be spotted relieving themselves just outside the line of lanterns with great ease, privacy and pleasure . . . precisely because they are not wearing panties.

The underwear manufacturers prefer to keep this quiet. Not only is it bad for business, it also suggests a primitive, if not heathen image to the outside world who invented the glories of assorted underwear. Panties at all times is good for everyone economically. Finally, it also provides a challenge for photographers of "Friday" and "Focus" magazines to try and capture on film what we all know exists but are not allowed to publish.

A final note: some women put on clean panties to go to bed in and keep the same pair on during the next day. This horrific idea should be treated with the contempt it deserves.

Why "Hello Kitty"?

The number of young women who wear "Hello Kitty" mittens is quite surprising. There are gloves as well. Usually persimmon red, there are yellow or mint green pastel English letters across the back near the knuckles with pastel hearts and flowers around a pastel kitten that is mostly face. Ask any wearers and (between giggles) they'll tell you they like the mittens because they are *kawaii.*

Well, we'll concede they are "cute" but can imagine many things far cuter. Further, it's hard to imagine that wearing them makes the wearer any cuter past the age of six. So there must be more to why sixteen year old to even twenty-six year old young ladies wear them.

Some market analysts suggest it has to do with Japanese perceptions of fashion itself. It is not until a girl marries or otherwise holds fantasies of actually buying haute couture before she actually notices it, they contend. Others, more street-wise, believe that fashion is determined by peers so that not until a peer group changes do fashions change.

Even though there are gloves that stretch from infant sizes to our rather large adult hands, aging alone should change peer group fashions in more than size. In modern Japan, puberty begins before 12 years of age. Ubiquitous TV promotion and near universal expectations for women should encourage fashion fantasies at an early age: 1) go on to college, 2) work long enough to find Mr. "Right" (still often decided by parental committee), 3) marry, 4) honeymoon abroad and 5) have children. (Remember "I dreamed . . . wearing my new 'Rubbermade' bra. . ."? Or was it 'Tupperwear'?) "Hello Kitty" must have some other reason to appeal in designer-conscious Japan — a place where somebody else's name on a bag is more important than the quality of the bag. Some crude macho types, as well as some joking Freudians, have suggested that Kitty is a semiconscious pun.

Such an explanation assumes a knowledge of English found until recently only in the Underground Dictionary (translated into Japanese near the turn of the decade — it is useless for learning underground Japanese since equivalents are not given — only explanations such as "slang for vagina" and the like). While there may be a germ of truth in all these explanations — sometimes only an infectious one, infectious for laughter — we think the answer can be found in "Hello Kitty" itself.

Kitty is a cartoon character aimed at young girls. It is usually used to promote girls' toys and products for ages from near infancy to elementary school and beyond. Its pre-puberty appeal is hardly reduced when a vast number of girls complete their education in exclusively girls' schools, including college. It is only natural that some normal Japanese girls will manifest the same results produced by convent schools in other countries. Indeed, there should be no surprise at all since Japanese all-girl schools are modeled on the convent and many have formal relationships with Roman Catholic institutions.

The students don't become Christians but do have a need to recall emotionally satisfying times from earlier in their lives. Kitty is at last cast aside when a marriage is of necessity arranged, but then only for a couple of years. Then the young mother can buy them again, pretending that all those cute little illustrated towels, hankies and assorted trinkets are really for her *kawaii* little baby.

Why Ankle Socks?

The Japanese fashion sense veers in all directions simultaneously, and the reasons just why particular people wear particular outfits are not always easy to fathom.

First, there is the unusual phenomenon of the latest Paris, London and New York fashions appearing overnight and in apish haste on the ready-to-wear hangers of *depāto* in vast and cheaper numbers. The logic behind this is very simple: if it's good enough to be ogled at as haute couture over there, it must be perfect for masse couture over here. There is an additional feature of international fashion shows — they use the time-honored Japanese theatrical convention of a walkway (*hanamichi*) right through the middle of the audience. They borrowed from us, so why shouldn't we borrow from them? No questions asked.

When it comes to personal, random use of Western styles, one begins to wonder what kind of objective fashion sense Japanese women possess. This is most apparent with hats. The standard, traditional Japanese proportions, male and female, have never really suited hats, or vice versa. The Oriental head tends toward the large and round, the body towards the truncated, so to speak. Neither of these characteristics is guaranteed to do justice to hats, especially large, floppy ones. Take samurai helmets, for example. They look fine in period films, but once you realize that the mighty Ieyasu was hardly more than a midget, and that his helmet was almost half his height again, then you begin to wonder if he could really have carried it off with dignity. Perhaps someone else carried it for him?

The same is roughly true of the modern Japanese woman who wants to look like Princess Diana. However, who are we to laugh? If she feels comfortable, trendy, confident, and even regal, that's fine — she doesn't have to look at herself, after all.

But how can we explain away that widespread phenomenon — the use of very short socks to add spice to fat legs? They're not only worn at the bottom of fat legs, of course, but for some masochistic reason the two characteristics often go together. Now, to us sock-culture people these look quite ridiculous and far from flattering in any sense, and yet Japanese find them *kawaii,* be they white, pink, yellow or pom-pommed. Clearly we are once again up against a difference in aesthetic perception. The Western idea is that shoe, sock (stockings, tights, etc.) and leg should be regarded as an entity, preferably full of enticement (and if not, better covered up altogether). The Japanese sensibility must be more selective: the beauty of the sock can be used to detract from the lack of leg appeal, in just the same way that any sensitive Japanese can easily appreciate a sunset while ignoring the mass of wires which spoil the view for us insensitives.

Why No Shoes?

The custom of taking your shoes off before entering a house is one that has given the Japanese an international reputation for cleanliness and hygiene — a reputation that is richly deserved, for who really enjoys the idea of people traipsing in off the street and wiping all the filth and nastiness from their shoes on to your nice, clean carpet?

Well, you may say, couldn't some ingenious inventor come up with an efficient, computerized doormat that would wipe shoes spotlessly clean, so that it wouldn't mess up the carpets? As far as it goes, that's a good idea, and it would certainly be welcomed by the manufacturers of lace-up shoes, whose Japanese market has always been sluggish because people are too lazy to keep lacing up and unlacing

their shoes as they enter and leave houses. But that's not all there is to it.

For one thing, many Japanese houses, or at least certain rooms in them, have no carpets, but instead have floors of *tatami* mats, which are made of rice straw, and are very sensitive to hard outdoor footwear, such as hobnailed boots, wooden *geta* clogs, and so on. Therefore, rather than submit all guests to embarrassing foot inspections (or sole-searching) for hard, un-*tatami*-friendly components, best to ban all shoes. Furthermore, the lace-up shoe lobby is small fry when compared with the interests that back the sock industry, and it is in the sock industry's interests that people should take off their shoes as often as possible. Not only will this make their socks wear out quicker, it will also make the wearing of clean, holeless socks essential for life in civilized society. After all, you can only wear socks with holes in if you've got shoes on and run no risk of being caught out.

Yet another industry that profits indirectly from this is the washing-machine manufacturers. Although Japanese people have advanced from the days when wearing clean socks was an ostentatious display of the fact that the wearer actually possessed a washing machine, now that everybody has one it has become even more important for anyone even remotely interested in his social standing to wear clean, fresh socks every day.

Then there is the cultural anthropological consideration. For hundreds, maybe thousands of years, the Japanese people have always drawn a strict distinction between outside the home and inside. And as it is the shoes that come into most direct contact with "outside," they cannot be permitted inside. Almost 1,000 years ago, Sei Shōnagon in her *Pillow Book* referred to shoes as "dirty things," and that attitude has become deeply ingrained in the Japanese ethos.

Therefore, if you have an accident at home and need to call the ambulance, make sure that your accident takes place near the door, so that the ambulance men don't need to waste vital seconds taking off their shoes to get to you, and then fumbling about under your stretcher to get them on again.

Why Slippers?

Why are slippers worn at the doctor's and dentist's? And why are they so worn out? They are threadbare at the heels, split at the sides and stained with what you can only hope is not blood or some particularly virulently diseased drop of some other bodily fluid. Hardly the image of spick-and-span cleanliness that you like to expect from medical practitioners.

You can see why they might not want you coming in with your shoes on and bringing with you more bugs and infection from the street. And if your doctor had deep Persian carpets laid in the waiting room, you could understand his concern for this expensive floor covering. But the place where most doctors keep their Persian carpets (which they can easily afford, of course) is normally their living room above the surgery. The waiting-room floor is a nice, cold, gray concrete, ideal for catching your death of cold through your feet.

So perhaps this provision of slippers is a philanthropic gesture to prevent feet from catching hypothermia during the long wait to be called. If that is so, we wish the philanthropy would stretch to providing a few cushions on the benches, too. But doctors and dentists, besides being notoriously rich, are also infamously stingy, and we suspect that that is one reason why they will not permit outdoor shoes: they are not willing to cough up the pittance to pay someone to sweep the floor occasionally, but feel bound by conscience to make a few grotty pairs of slippers available.

By making the slippers small on purpose, they ensure that patients' feet overlap the soles and their socks do the job of cleaning the floor, while actually paying the doctor his not unextravagant fee for the privilege of doing it.

We also smell a bit of collusion with the drug companies. Anyone who has walked past chemists' shops in Japan will note that the largest, most eye-catchingly revolting adverts are for hemorrhoid creams and athlete's foot cures. It is clear that the vast majority of hemorrhoids in Japan are the result of long hours spent waiting on a bench for the doctor to call you in and tell you that you have a cold. But you could never ask the doctor himself to cure those piles: it would be a rather snide insult to a respected member of the vertical society. And the same with athlete's foot. Those slippers must be a veritable breeding ground, crossroads, pan-national marketplace for highly infectious strains of itchy little fungi to spawn and attach themselves to the next unsuspecting foot, and the next, and the next, and the next. . . .

So roll up! Exchange your cold, or a bad tooth, or even a gallstone, for some piles and a nice case of athlete's foot. Keep the drug manufacturers in business, and support your local doctor, too, for we should not be surprised if he is handsomely rewarded by the drug companies for not providing cushions, and for providing those infection-ridden slippers.

Why Toilet Slippers?

These are specially to embarrass *gaijin,* as has often been remarked. A *gaijin* stands up from the *tatami* to go to the toilet, crosses the hallway in one pair of slippers and dutifully changes into another pair clearly marked "W.C." or some such slogan — but this *gaijin* invariably forgets to change back when he emerges. He may even forget to take his toilet slippers off when he re-enters the *tatami* room, thus committing not one but two social blunders simultaneously, and causing considerable mirth at his own expense.

After all, what is their purpose? It cannot be for you to avoid getting your feet dirty, for toilet slippers are always so dainty that even Cinderella would be hard put to fit her tiny feet into them; and the poor *gaijin's* feet often overlap so far that wearing the damn things is painful and he takes them off anyway.

It cannot be for hygiene, for surely nothing could be less hygienic than having several people an hour (at peak periods) donning the same slippers.

It cannot be for warmth, for the design of a Japanese toilet is such that no one could ever stay there long enough to worry about cold feet, as you might do if it was more suitable a place for taking along a good book. And anyway, most toilet slippers are made of very cold materials, often colored a pretty frigid blue.

There must be other purposes. And indeed there are. Several, in fact. One of them refers only to those tiny little ones made of a block of wood about 20 cm long with a little strap across the top, like baby Dr. Scholl's sandals. The wood of which they are made has a most resonant quality, and echoes really well against the tiled walls and floors of the smallest room. In this society where a polite silence is observed so ubiquitously, what greater pleasure than to escape once in a while to the privacy of the loo and kick up (literally) an infernal row? And you get the added attraction of hearing in stereo the echoes of that beloved sound of *geta* clacking down the street.

Another purpose is silent revenge. There is a story, doubtless totally and frivolously fictional, in a book called *The Three Bamboos,* of a Meiji Era Japanese Baron who served some Western guests of his a delicious meal in which human excrement had been cunningly mixed: this was to return an insult and satisfy his honor, the book explains. Well, most of us would not go to such lengths, but if, for example, you know that your boss or someone against whom you bear a grudge is about to go to the toilet (easy to tell by statistical analysis of amount drunk, who's already been and frequency of target person's fidgeting on his cushion), then you can nip in just beforehand and do unspeakable things to the toilet slippers.

If your victim notices, it will be too late. But even if he doesn't, honor will have been satisfied. ''Doctored'' toilet slippers have taken over in modern Japan from beheading followed by harakiri as a means of chivalrous revenge.

Why Scrape?

Why do people scrape their feet along the ground when they walk? Intolerant critics of this practice call it slovenly, and point scorn at the way so many wear their shoes squashed at the heels. But this is not surprising when you think of how often shoes have to be taken off and put on again when entering and leaving houses, public baths, medical institutions and even some offices. And note the obvious advantage of this way of walking: a people that trudges, flops and scrapes its way along the street is hardly good material for a military revival.

In fact, this phenomenon supports the theory of cultural habits being genetically programmed. For centuries, the Japanese wore *geta* (wooden clogs) or *waraji* (straw sandals). Lafcadio Hearn saw piles of the latter, worn out and discarded on the way up Mount Fuji; perhaps they are still there, under all the drink cans. Such footwear could not but be flopped and scraped along the ground, attached to the foot as it was merely by a thong between the toes. *Geta* used to make a characteristic sound: clip, clop, or click, clack, or however you want to express it. Actually, the English habit of changing the vowel in these onomatopoeic expressions is not always reflected in Japanese, so perhaps it should really be clop, clop, or clack, clack, or whatever. In any case, this sound remains dear to the Japanese breast, and although it is now rarely heard, on those occasions when the sound of *geta* does come echoing down the street it arouses in the Japanese *kokoro* (= heart, not ears) a nostalgic passion totally incomprehensible to the Western *kokoro,* or *mimi* for that matter.

Moreover, the mode of walking which suits clogs and produces these wonderful sounds is now genetically programmed into the Japanese *ashi* (a convenient term for both leg and foot), so that even when wearing jogging shoes, or those rain boots that people put on as soon as it starts to spot with rain, or those special black patent leather shoes for weddings, funerals and ballroom dancing, people still walk as if they wanted their Western-style footwear to emit those charming sounds as they walk down the street. Sounds are indeed emitted, but it is doubtful whether they really do charm the Japanese *kokoro* so much.

Of course, this also explains why there is so little mugging in Japan: no would-be thug has the skills of creeping up behind a would-be victim with the silence that is necessary for making a surprise attack. Thus, at the first scrape of sneaker against concrete, the victim can gather his wits about him and make good his escape — running so fast that he even forgets to scrape his feet along the ground.

Why Berets?

There seems to be a strong undercurrent in Japanese society of conformity, not so much in the general sense as pointed out by so many commentators, but rather of conformity to the look of what you either are or would like to be taken for. We can call this the uniform uniform syndrome. In other words, in Japan you are what you wear.

Japanese love uniforms at least as much as pin-striped British businessmen and cowboys do. The main difference is that Japanese like to wear their uniform of office even if that particular office is hardly worth wearing a uniform for. We all expect the great chefs of Europe to wear impressive chef's hats whether they be in Paris or selling their services to the great hotels of Tokyo. But it comes as a surprise to find your humble Japanese cook (unfortunately rendered as *cock-san*) in a hole-in-the-wall bistro in some anonymous suburb parading a chef's hat that clearly belongs in the Guinness Book of Records. Maybe he has great aspirations. Maybe he just likes to feel at one with the great. Whatever the reason, there is no chance we will confuse him with the gas-man. (He wears a gas-man's jacket.)

Take the not-so-humble Japanese cowboy. A contradiction in terms he may be, considering the lack of cows, but whether he be singing Country in Roppongi or rounding up a handful of steers in Hokkaido, he will have the complete outfit. Clint Eastwood beware.

So what about the beret? Well, once the Japanese discovered that there were fortunes to be made from abandoning black ink and woodblocks (at roughly the same time as the West was discovering them) and switching to oils and huge canvases, they needed a uniform to prove just who they were and how much they must be worth. This was hardly difficult to find. Paris was the only place to flock, and flock the overnight oil painters did. The beret was the obvious, if hardly original, choice of uniform: simple, very French and useful for keeping pigeons and paint off the pomade. To make it Japanese it became the *berē-bō* ("beret hat").

When these pseudo-Frenchmen return home after 60 years to lay their bones in the Motherland and get a good bowl of noodles, they are still wearing their *berē-bō*. Being painters and not photographers, they did not walk everywhere with "Autoboy" cameras, so, in the manner of Elizabethan voyagers, they are expected to act and dress appropriately to prove they have been, seen and painted . . . and are therefore entitled to huge prices.

There are young trendies who copy the uniform, but they are following French fashion, and must not be confused with the skilled octogenarian.

In conclusion, *berē-bō* = old man, probably artist, apprenticed in Paris, works not to be had cheap. *Berē-bō* come and go, reminiscing of Picasso.

Why Suits in Summer?

It is always one of life's mysteries when one culture assiduously assimilates something from another which has no real benefits to offer. The Western business suit is a classic example of this.

To a British businessman a suit makes sense. First, it can make the wearer look smart and well-coordinated, even sophisticated. Second, the cloth can be cut according to the purse and the season, bearing in mind that it rarely gets horrifically hot in Westminster. Third, the design is functional: pockets outside and inside and sufficiently strong to hold the heavy but valueless British coins.

But the Japanese had no need of any of that in summer, when the sweat oozes down even the skinniest back. Kimono may not have had real pockets, but they did have sleeves, and *haramaki* and *furoshiki* were equally useful, if not more so. And what better in summer than a loose-fitting *yukata* (the same principle as an Arab robe), the extent of leg covered depending on taste?

Enter the suit and necktie. Standard uniform, company feeling. A must for real moneymaking. Requiring long underwear when the legs get sticky. Basically too hot to wear outside in summer, and cumbersome to carry around, especially if everything falls out of the pockets. Hence the need to carry a small handbag as well: as long as everyone else does it, it isn't effeminate. Tie constrictive, shirt collar itchy, armpits sweaty — in fact, not very much good to be said about the suit at all. So why wear one? Why make it obligatory?

Fashion, perhaps? Yes, but most fashion designers don't

wear business suits. Training and discipline? Yes, but does it encourage more profits? International feeling? Yes, that must be it. Dress like them and they might be fooled into thinking that we really are the same as them. You are what you wear. Gentlemen wear suits, trustworthy people wear suits, solid workers wear suits, and who are we to argue?

Now we know we're not the same as them, and they suspect it, but they might believe in the suit. And we can go one step further by ordering British cloth to prove our interest in international trade harmony — well, get someone to bring it back for us, anyway.

And the tie? Perfect for proving how innocuous we really are as individuals, how lacking in originality and taste. Something for the hostess to buy us for Christmas ("Picked it up at the station").

But most important of all, where else are we going to stick the company lapel-pin if we don't have a lapel?

Why White Suits?

In Oshima's film *Gishiki* (Ceremony, 1971), there is a memorable scene where the ritualized Japanese wedding reception carries on regardless of the fact that the bride has jilted the groom. Black humor, nonsense, far-fetched? Not at all. Attend any formal Japanese wedding party and you will be treated to a host of absurdities, the bigger the wedding the more preposterous the rituals: speeches given when neither bride nor groom are present, endless speeches before anyone is allowed to have a drink, all species of alcohol served simultaneously, a giant plastic-cake-cutting ceremony, the tearful reunion with parents and new parents-in-law at the far end of the room, the groom in his white suit . . . . White suit? Why?

To be truly married in Japan (and whether you do it Shinto-style or in a church nobody really seems to care these days), you must have the big sit-down meal. A buffet is possible, but a bit cheap, really. Moreover, the food must be Western, so that all the relatives up from the country in their ill-fitting suits will feel even less at ease. And you must have as many costume changes for the bride and groom as the budget will allow. Forget all the Western trimmings at first — much better to launch off in kimono. But somewhere between the section chief's speech and the first college friends' chorus, there must come the Western attire.

Women can wear what they like — everyone will think it's wonderful, anyway — but the correct thing for the groom to wear in these decadent times is a white suit and frilly front. The reason for this is supposedly to persuade everyone that, whatever your relatives and schoolfriends are thinking, and however much your ex-girlfriends in the crowd are crying, you are really a pure and perfect person, destined to be a faithful and upstanding husband — at least for the first week. But the real reason is much deeper, much subtler than that.

It is a reason that is so subconsciously felt, that few could name it, but it epitomizes the wedding mish-mash. As you stand beside your bride, pretending to be so sweet and virginal, you can carry the candle from table to table with confidence and pride in your taste of rebellion. For beyond all the confused symbolism of white and purity and internationalism and unity and concord, for once in your life you can wear totally the wrong uniform and get away with it — yes, you can wear gangster clothes and nobody will raise an eyebrow.

V
Customs and Customers

Why Wedding Halls?

Simply because it's big business — too big to leave to temples, shrines and churches alone. Although recent figures show a decline in average expenses per wedding, income is still rising with the number of baby-boomers' children coming of age to marry, in their mid-to-late twenties. The fees from one wedding season (October through December) alone would pay for most buildings where they stand, in high-rent districts. (Not to mention that individual wedding expenses could have made homeowners out of the average newly wed!) At any rate, the remaining weddings scattered throughout the rest of the year are rich gravy indeed.

The origin of wedding halls actually is relatively recent. For not until the Meiji Restoration, which might more properly be called the 1868 Revolution, did most Japanese have a surname. And if the bride has no surname to begin with, how can the parents spend their life savings on celebrating her changing it? Only if she had chosen, or had had chosen for her, a samurai, a priest, or a rich merchant, could she have gained a new name — and people like that didn't need wedding halls because they had plenty of space for a ceremony at home.

Not only were names passed around after 1868, but also land and some basic rights like being able to eat the rice that one grew — white rice for every table and wedding registration for every household!

Unfortunately, spacious housing didn't always go with

the land, much less with contract employment. While anyone now had the right to have a splendid wedding fit for a noble, Everyman's home was not castle enough. There was a nearly instant market for something modeled on the Chinese wedding pavilion.

Along with the ''restoration'' and purification of the Imperial cult came the need to separate Shinto shrines (*jinja*) from Buddhist temples (*tera*). Many had shared the same grounds and facilities for centuries. Separation, however, tended to divide up life and death ceremonies. Whether it was with the flip of a coin or whatever, the *jinja* got life (naming babies and wedding ceremonies) while the *tera* got death (funerals and safe-keeping for the afterlife).

It is difficult to say which got the richer end of the bargain — impoverishing young couples before their life together gets started or raiding the stores that can't be taken into the afterlife. In any case, both rites of passage are more exorbitant than in most societies and sufficient to satisfy the needs of any family with the desire to make a grand show of wealth.

Of course, neither rite holds a complete monopoly. Christian churches (usually much cheaper and as grand a ritual as any) have become increasingly popular. Enough so as to raise the issue among Christians that they may be considered mercenary in performing wedding ceremonies for people who neither profess Christianity nor otherwise attend functions of the congregations providing such services.

Even elopements fail to threaten the wedding-hall business. More and more they are the place where receptions are held after the fact of marriage. Even year-old babies are handed about as toasts and wedding cake make the rounds among guests!

Why Christmas Cakes?

Japan's unique Christmas cake tradition is a modern mystery. Most Japanese don't know it is uniquely Japanese! Consequently, the answer about this drooly delight depends on who you ask. It is doubtful even to call it a tradition for, like so much of japonaiserie moderne, Christmas cake is most certainly a postwar phenomenon.

Most Japanese seem to think Christmas cake came from America. This opinion seems corroborated by Jehovah's Witnesses (who actually did first come from America) by their denying it along with birthday cake for their children; for them, as for Jack Benny — possibly anyone at some time, birthdays are anathema.

Many Christian missionaries of more conventional persuasion likewise disparage Japanese commercialization of Christmas and seem to corroborate the idea of some confusion of celebrating Christ's birthday with birthday cake to explain the ex nihilo materialization of a near Satanic temptation to gluttony. Deadly sin aside, Japanese "authorities" responsible for articles in Japanese encyclopedias flatly state the tradition came from America (North, South, Central? . . . at least it is easy to see why such "authority" deserves scant respect).

Compelled by curiosity, we have pieced together the

following from old-line bakers, advertising execs, personnel directors and teachers. During the difficult times during and shortly after U.S. occupation, Christmas afforded a rare opportunity for companies to give a party for their employees en masse as they normally were expected to do near the year's end: a little more to eat, a lot more to drink — and some ordinary cake left over to take home in a napkin to share with the family.

Bakeries became an institution in rice-eating Japan through contracts to supply bread for school lunches (the cheapest way to supply needed calories and nutrition nationwide). With improvement of the economy, cake soon became more than a seasonal item; to keep pace and not lose the seasonal market, Christmas cake soon became more elaborate. No expense was spared in eventual promotion (and making) so that prices continue to range from about $10-$75. After 1984, what used to be a one-day children-only specialty item came to be a ten-day grown-up children's item in any home with a new generation of school-age children. Come Christmas Day, however, not a cake — not even non-spoiling do-it-yourself kits — can be found on a store's shelf anywhere!

Inquiries by gluttonous bargain-hunting *gaijin* revealed that they did not all turn into pumpkins. The horrifying fact is that nearly all Christmas cakes end up being THROWN AWAY!! Not sold off cheap, not given away to orphanages, not fed to pigs, but thrown away. It seems that the Christmas spirit is so alien to Japan that merchants (who wouldn't mind more favorable publicity in the whole affair) have no appropriate recipients: such gifts are spurned as insults. Even beggars refuse any charity that would ''prove'' them to be dependent and so inferior.

But, drool, *gaijin* aren't Japanese, so, er, hmm!

Why Valentines?

Given the keen Japanese nose for marketing opportunities, it is interesting to see what has happened to St. Valentine's Day. As in the West, Valentine's Day is essentially a merchants' holiday created by advertising and sales promotions and maintained by susceptible masses. Well, then, why not Easter, too? After all, if Christmas can be such a success, Easter must be a natural — you know, bonnets, parades, home videos and chocolate Easter bunnies with jellybeans. . . .

Let's first take a look at the success of Valentine's Day in Japan. The only pagan tradition for Valentine's Day is the same for Japanese as it is for the rest of the world: the Roman festival to the god Lupercus (Pan) in mid-February. If later questions about Valentine's Christian sainthood have posed no threat to declarations of love concretely sealed with material gifts in the West, they're a non-issue in the East.

What has been at issue, however, is how to promote the day for maximum profits. To date, the most successful have been confectioners with their sale of chocolates. While the materials for making traditional Valentine cards have not been promoted with any success, there are kits for making your own chocolate valentine.

But what a twist fate has wrought! The chocolate companies realized that Japanese men do little or no shopping and any initial campaign to get the attention of their feudal mentality would be futile. Any indirect approach would be equally ill-advised. Hence, the woman buys the valentine for the man!

The initial promotion succeeded in getting office girls to recognize the necessity to declare fealty to their macho mentors and overlords, which in turn was reinforced by their bosses' expecting such gifts as a matter of course. The backlash that might have been expected when the truth leaked out has failed to materialize.

In spite of some grumbling by the younger and lower-paid, it is as one OL (office lady) explained, "the best obligatory gift time ever. We buy them the best chocolates we can find — ones we'd never buy for ourselves; we go in together so it is really a nice gift. But most men don't enjoy chocolates. After they open it and get a good whiff, they give it back to us!"

And — oh, these wily merchants — they have added a second Valentine's Day in March: "White Valentine's Day" just one month later. The Year of the Rabbit — 1987 — may not have marked the year of the Easter Bunny, but it did have two Valentine's Days scheduled in Japan.

Why White Day?

Well, imagine. What would you do with a mountain of white chocolate? Past marketing of white chocolate in

Japan hasn't been much more successful than anywhere else. It simply doesn't taste as good as "real" chocolate.

Further, while you can cheat by using other fats and oils in producing an edible but cheaper dark chocolate, white chocolate needs more genuine (and expensive) cocoa butter to be at all acceptable. A lot is passed off as a genuine regional sourvenir of Hokkaido. (Never mind that chocolate comes from tropical climes — we have the Swiss, Dutch, even Hershey, Pa., don't we?) But the demand for souvenirs doesn't seem to be able to sustain prices anywhere near production capacity.

Oh, to repeat the success of Valentine's Day! — Why not? This time for men to buy for women. This is a small market since only young and unmarried men still do any shopping . . . but, like their elders, they don't really appreciate chocolate, so it is relatively easy to pawn off the white stuff. Appropriately enough, the new "tradition" was launched in 1984. Beware the Ides of March — and here's mud in St. Pat's eye for good measure — for the original St. Valentine's tradition is carried over a month late to March 14.

But this time, the white theme has attracted more than the dairy industry's chocolate confectioners. The struggling textile industry unloaded white panties the following year — along with English inscriptions where many keep their knowledge of English anyway. Boys will be boys, right? . . . so at least some white chocolates must be included to symbolize pure intentions, shouldn't they?

While it may look like innovation of the most im-aginative kind to the Western mind, what makes it accep-

table to the Japanese is the knowledge they are carrying out some long standing tradition. Of course, the authority to consult to understand such tradition must be Japanese. The Western mind can't interpret for Japanese.

Just look at the problems posed by Easter. The Japanese realize the Easter bunny's schedule is ''something like Jewish Passover or Muslim Ramadan, using a lunar calendar — we know something about such calendars from our own — but it's lunacy to ask Westerners to explain how it works. They have no appreciation of what we need in the domestic market but insist on giving us lectures in religion and how they are all entirely different and why theirs is right and on and on dogmatically contradicting each other. It's all so irrelevant when we know how we want to observe tradition anyway!''

There may be something to such an attitude, given the other choices for a March holiday. Does anyone celebrate the Ides? Do the Irish drink green beer on the 17th, or

Guiness? Must we? So never fear about Easter being taken over. But then who knows? Chocolate eggs and rabbits have already made off-season appearances; Easter Bunnies are bound to follow. But they may be transfers from old Playboy Clubs.

Why *Meishi?*

It would be nice to say that the name-card tradition was an ancient one stretching back to an age where samurai bowed low, sucked their teeth and exchanged bits of bark or tortoiseshell or rice paper with their names engraved upon them. But it is not so. The fact of the matter is that this is a foreign import, copied from 19th century Westerners who used visiting cards. This habit was quickly pounced upon by the Japanese as an aspect of civilization and enlightenment, and as a good way to promote the new paper industry, whose foundations had then just been laid at Oji. And they never looked back.

But there is one aspect that goes back to the samurai: once you have someone's *meishi*, you are bound and obliged to that person for the rest of your life. You have to do otherwise unthinkable things like give up the chance of a seat in the train, or stand back in the stampede for the last taxi, or apologize deeply when he pokes his umbrella in your eye. Such are the duties of receiving the name card of another.

One misconception must, however, be nipped in the bud: the purpose of a name card is not, repeat not, to help others remember your name. When you have a card printed, you conventionally put your name in the middle, but that is not where the recipient looks first. He looks at the much, much more important information hiding away in one corner: your company, and your position in which department and which section. Only then will he know "who" you are, and know whether to toady up to you or to patronize you. You only have your name printed big in the middle of the card to try and distract his attention from the lowly name of your insignificant company, and the humble position you occupy in its least successful division; but the ploy never works, and the critical perusal of your embarrassing details soon evokes some more teeth-sucking and a withering, *"Ah, so desuka? Ah, ha, ha, ha."*

On the other hand, if you do work for a prestigious company, you make sure that its logo is ostentatiously displayed in an upper corner, preferably in color. Then the *"Ah, so desuka?"* receives a different intonation altogether, as your new-found friend tries to tell you how many very, very good friends he has in one of your branches, (The cousin twice removed of his wife's elementary school teacher's divorced brother-in-law's second wife once went to an *o-miai* arranged marriage introduction meeting with a university graduate who had done part-time vacation work delivering parcels for its Aomori sub-branch.) and plies you from then on with extravagant gifts twice every year.

Never have a name card printed with only your name on it. It will be treated with extreme suspicion, not to say outright hostility.

Why *Hanko?*

There is nothing harder to fake than, dare we say it in these troubled times, a fingerprint. What's more, as long as you still have the finger attached to you, it is the perfect means of identification, always to hand. All that is required is ink, mud or blood.

But in Japan, for Japanese anyway, it is only used when all else is missing. "All else" means just one thing: the *hanko*, variously translated as stamp, seal or chop. The personal seal is the one means of identification Japanese really believe in: I stamp, therefore I am.

But, you may well ask, what is wrong with the signature? One simple thing wrong with it is that most other nations use it, and it would never do to fit in too much with the rest of the world. But there is also the problem of how to write one's name. A true *kanji* signature should be written vertically, because it looks better that way. Unfortunately, most documents these days, except house contracts, tend to be printed horizontally. The alternative, therefore, is the *romaji* signature.

Romaji signatures present a problem of a different kind. They really don't come naturally to the average Japanese, and this means that foreigners are regularly being asked to "design" a good signature, and that of course destroys any element of originality, which is the idea of a signature in the first place. However, such Japanese are wise enough to know that their unaided signature looks rather like a high school writing exercise. The other thing of which they are often aware is that illegibility is a feature of the Western signature, and that leads logically to the conclusion that an illegible *kanji* signature is infinitely preferable and less troublesome. After all, who is going to be impressed by your English writing ability if your writing is unintelligible?

No, *hanko* are the thing, despite the obvious hassle and expense of having one made so that it cannot easily be copied, and the problem of how easy it is to lose or forget it. And if someone else does acquire and use it, they become you!

Let us summarize the main reasons for still using *hanko*:

1. Most Japanese documents in daily use have small round circles into which your seal should roughly fit, and into which signatures definitely do not. Think of the expense of reprinting everything.

2. A *hanko* retains Oriental flavor.

3. *Hanko* craftsmanship is a traditional art, and we should keep the craftsmen working.

4. Similarly, think of all those people who deal with the registration of ''official'' *hanko*.

5. *Hanko* help to prove just how foreign foreigners are: without one you are only half a person. Conversely, if a foreigner does possess one, he is immediately suspect — why doesn't he or she use a signature?

6. It is convenient for the Emperor, as it saves the embarrassment of anyone asking for his signature. As his highest-rank seal weighs several kilos anyway, it also means that someone else can wield it for him and save him effort.

7. It is great fun on TV when police dramas can resort to huge blow-up pictures of suspect *hanko*, as presumably the real police sometimes do.
8. Red ink is attractive.

The *hanko* lives on. But the Japanese are also good at hedging their bets, and now, in hot pursuit of the combined *soroban*-calculator comes the true "sign pen" — half pen, half *hanko*. And that should avoid all confusion.

Why Slow Banks?

Service is slow in Japanese banks because they are not logical — it's "the Japanese way." You might expect them to at least be logical in their own interest in the way people who work with profits and losses are supposed to be cold, calculating and practical. But this is to overlook the arch-conservatism of banks — especially in Japan. When you combine "we always have done it this way" with "leading the way into the 21st century" you can only get absurd inconsistencies — lots of them.

Just when automation reduces total man-hour requirements, do banks reduce their new hires, expand service or provide more personal time and days off? Or use computers to handle job assignments and complex schedules? No way! Increase new hires, cut down banking hours and create make-work jobs like coming in early to punch doorbells to hand out calendars and tissues just as most families are trying to get off to school and work on time.

Besides, what would the standing committee to reduce Saturday services do at the Wednesday luncheon meeting of the Japan Bankers' Association if everyone decided to follow the world trend toward 24-hour service 365 days a year?

Does staff training provide universal understanding of longstanding but underutilized services such as checking? No way! Study the abacus and how to count past ten without using your toes (or why the Oriental — read "Japanese" — way of counting starting with the thumb is superior to the Occidental — read "American" — way starting with the index finger).

Besides, how else could a lowly clerk get the pleasure of refusing ignorant *gaijin* and sending them on wild goose chases to other departments and branches if they simply agreed to cash their own bank's checks on the spot? How else could *gaijin* get to know the Japanese way?

Should banks be expected to use modern means to make it more difficult to cash stolen bankbooks or to forge documents to transfer funds? No way! That is why they insist on personal seals that can be used by any hand.

Change the equipment but don't change procedures to take advantage of it. No, have those who use signatures write down a "secret" number that any clerk can read (and reserve for future use); there is no point in making it harder to steal or to forge things . . . what would supervisors have to justify their round-the-clock observation of their underlings?

We wouldn't want robots watching and recording, would we? Or rested, alert employees who would not have to work late hunting for fatigue-caused errors, would we?

Certainly nothing can be gained by internationalization of procedures in Japan — things would become too simple, while thieves would have to become more creative. That just wouldn't be the Japanese way to do banking.

Why the Abacus?

The current generation of bank clerks doesn't know how to use an abacus with accuracy and speed. But at the same time, the older generation doesn't know how to use anything else. Retraining is not very appealing to traditional minds, and so let's make the younger ones take *soroban* lessons! Thus, in spite of Japan's world leadership in producing electronics for banking and calculating, Japanese bankers lag far behind in adopting and using even hand calculators.

Like most businesses, banks have taken up slogans for entering the 21st century, but like the Ministry of Education, seem the least inclined to take the essential steps. Until recently it was enough to count yen and dollars; variable economic relationships and internationalization on a global scale, however, have gone far beyond the range of the adding-subtracting-multiplying-dividing *soroban*.

While most businesses must put college graduates into special training to bring them up to date, many banks are putting them into training to learn pre-19th-century skills and 19th century conceptualization of banking services. Simple division is cumbersome while time factoring, roots and probability calculation are alien concepts, impossible to do.

Banks requiring such training rationalize their approach with such justifications of MacArthur's judgment of the Japanese (like 12 year olds) as "what if the electricity failed?" They conveniently forget that even cheap credit card-size calculators have solar cells, so that even batteries are no problem, not to mention that whatever might decommission all computers would be nothing short of World War III. Any disaster on a scale to put banks even temporarily out of business will be way beyond the range of *soroban*. High-power computers with thousands of calculations per second and long distance hook-ups will be essential. Anything less can get by with fingers and toes (if they are still there).

The Ministry of Education must certainly be held responsible for encouraging the *soroban* mentality. Just as the government was adopting slogans for the 21st century and on the eve of education reform, it created special higher grades to license abacus training schools for children. This just precisely when it should have given a five-year advance warning that it would cease requiring any license to teach abacus and start requiring one for teaching computers and calculators to all ages.

The handwriting should have been on the wall (blackboard?) for all to see.

But don't misunderstand. There's nothing wrong with abacuses — just reliance on them in banks when people need sharpening of their computer and calculator skills. Abacuses are great tools for teaching number concepts to small developing minds. Also, exceptional skill in their use is as wonderful (and useful) as the ability to piece jigsaw puzzles together in jig time — but even here, with proper preparation, computers can do it faster.

Why *Obi?*

Japan is probably the only country in the world to hand out awards for the best-written "copy" on the slip of paper wrapped around a book to encourage purchase. Not only that — there are writers who specialize in writing that kind of blurb. Strange indeed. But why is the *obi* needed in the first place?

Let's look at what happens in other countries. The norm seems to be to have some kind of sticky label if you wish to announce that the record in question is a big hit, or the book is a best-seller, winner of some literary prize or, most commonly, being sold at a discount.

That is clearly not simple enough for the Japanese. Instead, they prefer to wrap this paper belt round the product, which immediately gets messed up when you try to stick the record in between other records, or the book on the shelf. An ignorant foreigner might destroy the *obi* at once, not realizing that the value of a second-hand record or book actually increases if still in the original *obi*, just as Dinky Toys are worth more if still in the original box. The only illogicality here is that the record jacket itself is the original "box."

So what is the reason? Well, as you would expect, it all

began with the egg. Eggs have been one of man's problem products over the ages because of their fragility, but the Japanese managed not only to perfect a means of safely wrapping and transporting eggs, they even made it into an art form. Then came the book. Once competition for book sales became fervent in a nation with an amazing literacy rate, it seemed a good idea not to leave everything to the salability of the author's name. Why not pay some other distinguished personage to write a brief blurb and create more work by having this message printed separately from the book as a mini work of art in itself?

The beauty of this system is that it fits in so well with the Japanese love of wasting paper and wrapping anything just one more time to make sure. It also fits well into the "form not content" syndrome: who knows how many books have been sold for their *obi* and never opened and read?

Then came the LP record. The problems here were slightly different. Being a nation of space-savers, the Japanese have always squeezed as many LPs as possible into one display box, making it almost impossible to flip each record forward, as in Western shops, so that you can look at the whole jacket of the next record. Instead a special flip-up-glance-drop-flip-up-next-record technique is required, and it is well worth watching experts for a few minutes in any record shop when you're at a loose end.

Only a moment's thought will show that unless the LP jacket bears useful written information right along the top, the flipper will have no idea what record he is flipping. This will necessitate a double flip and waste valuable seconds which could be better spent in a *pachinko* parlor.

Enter the *obi*. If well-designed, there will always be attractive information on the record's contents starting from the top — so that even a casual flip by an expert will reveal enough. Once the interest is aroused, and the record is withdrawn from the stack, then you can also have any information needed about the record, whatever the design on the cover may be. Clever, eh? Moreover, the *obi* information may be truly informative, telling you what kind of music or group is involved, just in case you don't know. Yes, *obi* can even be educational!

A silly sales gimmick at first glance, the *obi* turns out to be a fine combination of sales promotion technique and informative customer service. The moral: whether you read them or not, don't throw them away.

Why No Bargain Basements?

Because most department stores have food departments in their basements. Foreigners, however, seldom find bargains in these departments. Veterans imagine they find bargains in things as varied as wine and cheeses to sausages and pasta, but these souls are to be pitied for they obviously have not been outside Japan for some time.

Indeed, one begins to wonder if bargains are ever to be found in department stores outside the times when owners of winning baseball teams gather new fans by victory celebration sales at their affiliated stores. One year it's only a few stores in Tokyo; another year a few in western Japan; another year many stores in greater Tokyo and neighboring districts while Kyushu and other areas have neither winners nor teams with affiliated department stores.

Actually, "bargains" can be had after New Year's and in midsummer in the various *depāto* — if *bargain* can be the right term. Certainly it cannot normally be a verb in Japanese, and adjectival usage is uncertain. The noun can apply to either good or bad bargains and, in that sense, is valid. Often, merchandise is specially purchased for these sales with clearance items thrown in — from the warehouse, or even other stores.

Yet there is a counterpart to U.S.-style bargain basements as well as the widespread street or sidewalk sale. The latter are often called "cargo" or cart sales, whether they appear on the street or not. Some are organized affairs held seasonally as in Ginza or various building complexes. Others like bookstores or supermarkets have constant or regular clearances. Typically, some department stores and most supermarkets put dated bread and other perishables in bins or baskets ("cargo"). To get these bargains, be ready at the door before opening time and prepare to elbow past bag-ladies and impoverished missionaries gathering half-priced manna — often unsold leftovers are just what's preferred by *gaijin*, including whole wheat bread, low/high-fat milk, hard cabbages, red tomatoes and ripe melons. Following or at the end of the last traditional days to visit cemeteries, selected flowers and/or cute baskets of fruit are available at very low prices.

All such sales are genuine distress sales and are not used as come-ons to get you to look for more inside, nor are they in the spirit of Christmas. The status-conscious should not be caught buying or conspicuously using "cargo" merchandise — especially leftovers from graves (whether they actually got there or not). Bargain-floor goods, however, are not so risky, but are far from street level, usually just below the restaurant floors near the top of the store building. Here, it is best to do as the Romans warned even if it *is* Tokyo or Osaka: *Caveat emptor!*

Why No Bargaining?

The Japanese don't bargain and haggle because they don't have to. The distribution system as well as public expectations make it unnecessary to compete at the retail level. Consequently, no bargaining: just take it or leave it. (Did someone say "shove it!"?)

The distribution system is essentially feudal, or, in modern times, more properly labeled a successful form of fascism. That is not to say the Japanese government is Nazi, but like all right-wing governments it does assign, through various mechanisms, various segments of the economy to private enterprise.

Be that mechanism a "window of guidance" (official recommendations to industries, traders and economic institutions) or the controversial "designated bidder" system, there is little either open or "competitive" in the economy. Even small retailers are protected by regulation of the floor space allowed potentially competitive department stores and chain retailers. Traditional and historical ties or "connections" preserve the feudal character in assignments of the economy, and provide those solid non-tariff barriers that make it easy for the government to protest that it really is trying to liberate foreign imports, while keeping them uncompetitively high-priced.

Consequently, "bargaining" covers everything from distribution territory to conditions of payment only at the levels of higher management. In the end, these "gentlemen's agreements" are seldom committed to paper but remain more or less binding, so that by the wholesale level there is little to say other than "how much?"

This does not mean bargaining is out of the picture, but some understanding of the system is needed to find the best opportunities to go against traditional expectation. For example, shops devoted to one line of appliances seldom can bargain. They hold merchandise on consignment and have as little as a ten percent margin. They seldom can bargain without changing terms of consignment.

Department stores are a mixed bag with consigned and owned merchandise, and may bargain occasionally. Items with prices or totals that approach ¥100,000 can sometimes be had with savings up to 30 percent. Look for imports or previous sale lines or quantity purchases. (We've got wine, cheese, tailored clothing, kimono, furnishings, even real estate and leases this way, not to mention the usual photographic and electronic goods.)

Outright purchasing makes discount centers potential places to bargain, but their limited access to the normal wholesale system reduces competition among themselves so that discount prices become standardized as well.

In any case, it is essential to talk to the person with the

power to decide. Unfortunately, the process of finding that person can require time and some Japanese language ability that you must use yourself, since few Japanese have the inclination or capacity to bargain even in their own behalf. Thus, unless you are looking for practical Japanese lessons at a discount, the return in savings on time spent can be low wages indeed.

Why Greeters?

There used to be more than there are now — elegantly uniformed young ladies at the entrances to department stores bowing deeply, smiling at the floor and wishing customers welcome in silly squeaky voices. Bow, smile, greet; bow, smile, greet. . . .

Promotion brings with it the privilege of standing at the bottom of an escalator, further away from the drafty entrance doors that are never closed even when heating or air conditioning are going full blast. A further perk of this promotion is the great responsibility of holding in your slim, white-gloved hand a cloth for cleaning the handrail. Bow, smile, greet, wipe; bow, smile, greet, wipe. . . .

The bow also serves as a natural barrier to prevent too many customers from boarding the escalator at the same time. And the cloth is a fine instance of how differently Japanese people regard the hands and feet: they wear filthy toilet slippers but carefully wash their hands afterwards; and doctors don't mind their patients catching athlete's foot while department stores go to these great lengths to

protect their customers from hand infections transmitted by escalator handrails.

All these greeters also have a salutary effect on the nation's employment statistics. Every bank or store or other institution that employs even a single greeter deals a valuable blow in the cause of Japan's claim to be the only advanced nation to have no unemployment problem. Keynesian economics actually works here, although we doubt whether it was greeters that were uppermost in the great man's mind when he wrote of the importance of full employment.

But you don't see so many of them any more. Those of us who used to think of them as a silly institution, and used to tease them by standing at the bottom of the escalator and bowing back equally deeply, now regret that they have in many places been replaced by taped announcements or simulated voice machines. To the management, these odious contraptions have many advantages: they need no uniforms or tea breaks or shift rotations; they always sound equally cheerful; and indeed their voices can be made even more ridiculously squeaky just by speeding the tape up a bit. And the redundant greeters can find jobs assembling voice simulators, or recording the actual tapes, so there's no rise in the unemployment figures.

But speaking as customers, we feel that if there has to be a greeting at all, it should be by a real human, rather than a little electronic box, no matter how clever it might be at judging whether you are coming or going and saying *"irasshaimase"* or *"arigato gozaimashita"* accordingly.

VI
Habits and Habitats

Why High Voices?

Cosmetic cultural variations are fascinating to observe, as long as you are not on the receiving end of a lot of unnecessary discrimination simply because you were born either with or without certain distinguishing characteristics. The worst thing to be is resident somewhere where what you happen to possess is aesthetically unacceptable.

A good example of this is freckles. Now a goodly covering of those attractive little skin blemishes could make you a big star in Oklahoma or the Orkneys, but it could ruin your life in Osaka. There are even TV commercials in Japan advertising special cream with which to cover them in favor of a boring, unattractive pasty-faced mask.

Protruding fangs, or *yaeba* as they are known in Japan, are another good example. Now these are very much "in," or rather sticking out, in Tachikawa and Transylvania, but they are horrifying in Tennessee or Telford.

But there is another aspect of female acceptability or rejection which also shows regional variations, and that is the nature of the "attractive" voice. What we are talking about here is not the normal speaking voice, which comes in all volumes and tones as it does anywhere else in the world, but rather the public announcement voice. Most public announcements in Japan are female, and they have a unique timbre to them which is no doubt most attractive to Japanese of both sexes. To the average Western listener, it is a sound that seems sickly-sweet and grating, often teeth-grinding, sometimes spine-tingling and basically a pain in the ears.

The strange intonations of the Shinkansen announcer would come into the first category; most "*Irasshaimase*" voices would fit all categories.

Perhaps the most annoying feature of these voices is the artificiality of the whole thing — quite normal women with normal, pleasant voices somehow forced to speak in the way expected of them. But who decided on the "type" of voice for announcing, and using what criteria? Are we supposed to be soothed, in much the same way as babies are supposed to like the endless "*kawaii!*"'s hurled at them? Do men like the patronizing tones of women just one step away from vocal hysteria? Or is it that there is something "cute" about this kind of voice itself, in the same way that brainless, out-of-key young female singers are cute?

That must be it. *Yaeba* are cute, and so are moles on the face — but not freckles. And Japanese "cuteness" verges on suppressed sexuality. Certainly, if Japanese strippers are anything to go by, there is a big cultural divide when it comes to ideas of what is "sexy."

A Tokyo talent agency specializing in foreign voices was once asked to provide a "sexy" female voice for a TV commercial. A foreign agent found an American girl with the huskiest, sexiest voice imaginable. The girl with the voice arrived at the studio and turned out to be exactly what the Japanese directors didn't want. Instead the girl had to be coached by a Japanese female narrator to do a "sexy" high-pitched Japanese-style voice.

But that still begs the question of why anyone needs a sexy female welcome as you walk into a department store.

Why So Virginal?

Why do so many Japanese girls claim to be virgins? The unexpectedly simple answer to this is that many of them are — and often still are at an advanced age — despite what all the newspapers tell us about the high school kids of the Eighties.

Let us examine the genuine ones first. They are sometimes so by choice, sometimes as the simple result of strict parental care, but more often because of the obsession with going on group outings, often without members of the opposite sex, and also as a result of spending too much time in beauty salons.

The virgin by choice is waiting for a soap commercial man to bowl her over on a tropical island (two nights, three days) in the sunset and in slowmotion. Not in a love hotel. Not in a 4.5-mat dormitory. Not in the manager's private office—he hasn't got one anyway. Mr. Right can only be right, and of course he will want to deflower, nature conservation being what it is in Japan. So it goes.

The virgins by lack of opportunity have no excuse.

Now we come to the virgins by name. The pushing of the "Virginal Is Cute" image is rife, particularly by Takarazuka starlets dressed up as men and *kawaii-ko* singers dressed up as virgins. The popularity of this image leads to the technical virgin who is not exactly virginal in reality: no fuss, no mess, no risk, but yes please, anything else fine as long as nobody else sees it happening. The anxious Japanese male may find this situation trying and the female hard to explain away as there is a language problem — in Japan, the all-encompassing word SEX has had its richness whittled down to the crude meaning of "no-holds barred total act."

Also confusing to the poor male is the universal love of nun, nurse, stewardess and schoolgirl uniforms. Japanese panderers know well enough that because none of these professions is supposed to do it on the job, the image they purvey becomes perfect for arousing the dormant Yang and making it pay lots of money for the privilege. The logical result of this is that no men really believe in virginal appearance actually equating with virginal behavior. This is particularly confusing to the foreign male confronted by a 25-year-old in a pink 12-year-old party dress.

But then there are the rest who just pretend for convenience's sake that they have never been within a *tatami*-width of a close encounter of any kind. The results of lay experts in the field suggests that this category is indeed large. Why the white suits and dresses, the white candles, and the peculiarly-named *bājin rōdo* which leads up to the altar? Because we want to appear pure. Their Royal Highnesses the Duke and Duchess of York, hardly the best candidates for the no-sex-before-marriage stakes, would certainly have been amused to hear the endless repetition of the phrase during the live, peak-time Japanese TV coverage of their big day.

Which brings us to a final category, of course. The girls who actually have a chance of a place in the Imperial Family. No pretending there — for that job you have to be certified.

Why *Nozoki?*

Japan has never been noted for its love of privacy. *Nozoki* (peeping) is a national pastime. Hotel doors have gaps above them; partitions only stop drafts, not sounds; neighbors are always spilling the beans to private detectives; infrared lenses probe the night; the scandal magazines proliferate.

Although basic curiosity about one's fellow men is a human trait around the globe, the extent to which privacy is denied in Japan must be a result of a traditional lack of space and the construction of houses for flexibility rather than insulation. This made the *ninja* occupation an easy one, and it still means that blackmail and industrial spying are rife. For many foreigners, it is quite embarrassing to have to conduct quite important financial transactions in what can only be regarded as a public place. This may be a restaurant where all kinds of people can overhear, a club where other customers and the hostesses can all hear, or even a "private" Japanese restaurant where the waitresses are never out of earshot.

This no doubt makes the work of police detection that much easier. The concept of "minding your own business" hardly applies and the love of watching other people through a television camera or through the frames of cartoon magazines reflects this attitude.

It is not always easy to distinguish curiosity from voyeurism. Many foreigners find questioning from strangers about their weight, age, marital status and salary quite unnerving and unnecessary, if not downright rude, but Japanese put it down to mere curiosity. But a streak of voyeurism runs through a lot of television programs and magazines.

It has to be something to do with the lack of excitement in people's lives, and the desire to experience different things which often can only be done secondhand. In a way, though, it is this very vicarious approach which appeals, and ties in with the Japanese dislike of getting involved directly in other people's affairs. Watch the neighbors and talk to others about them, but don't get too close. Watch the stripper through a peephole or talk to her over the telephone, but avoid actual contact. Dress up in black and prowl around in the bushes to watch others making love rather than getting on with it yourself. Steal panties off lines rather than buy them yourself (men, that is). And so it goes on.

All these things only serve to underline the traditional Western view of the Oriental as unfathomably two-faced, certainly amoral if not actually immoral.

But if we see the other side of this, it could be just another way of avoiding the inevitable stresses of a packed society. And if the end result is less murder, less rape, fewer sex crimes and more police contact, then it can't all be bad.

Why Comic Violence?

Because violence is interesting and amusing, even; it shouldn't be surprising to find it in Japanese *manga* comic books. Generations who were raised on the Three Stooges or the Marx Brothers, tell war stories and enjoy Looney Tune Cartoons know that, don't they? That's to say Japanese comics don't seem more violent than, say, classics like Krazy Kat, Katzenjammer Kids or contemporary flicks like *Star Wars, Rambo, The Terminator* or similar PG fare from the States.

Coupled with the common observations that there is less violent crime in Tokyo contrasted with New York, Detroit, even London or Sydney, not to mention Ulster, Soweto or Watts, the combined perspective on Japanese comics gives currency to Aristotle's concept of catharsis. While Aristotle's theory was applied only to high tragedy, Japanese comics seem confined to basic Anyman if not Everyman.

Psychologists don't agree while social psychiatry seems more art than science, but in any case it is certainly preferable to have Japanese violence in Japanese *manga* than in Chinese cities or Pacific islands outside Japanese territorial waters. Still, a chicken-and-egg argument stands in apposition to the cathartic approach.

Certainly there is support for either (A) *manga* are a manifestation of existing violence or (B) an inspiration for its continuation. Analysts in both camps cite such facts as much of Japanese violent crime goes unreported. For some (more so than in most Western countries), rape is a tradition rather than a crime — even as a crime, quite differently understood from place to place or "case by case," so that racist Mississippi and liberal Illinois judges seem more consistent by comparison. Of course, everyone cites bullying in schools (by teachers as well as students), traditional out-of-court settlement, overturning of convictions based on police ''extracted'' confessions and acceptance of beating down the nail that sticks up in society.

Certainly, no one disputes Japanese excellence in the martial arts or the nature of Kabuki exuberance. Yet, the varieties of football on both sides of the Atlantic, ice hockey and Hollywood reveal the dangers of a one-sided approach.

But surely a balanced view of Japanese comics reveals less violence than many choose to focus upon. Comic illustration goes back nearly a millenium, including a famous Buddhist scroll featuring farting frogs and cavorting hares. (Or is it cavorting frogs and farting hares?) The tradition blossomed with woodblock printing a century ago and boomed from a few decades ago starting with both social and political satire in the Sixties; fantasy caught on in the Seventies, while comic parody seems to characterize the Eighties. Classics are still to be found in the making while some early ones dating from Occupation times continue to the present, find their way into serialized TV, get translated and are even on video cassettes. None of these feature violence any more than Disney.

As for the violence that can be found, if an Aristotelian catharsis of some sort does not apply at the time of reading, old *manga* exchanged for 30 meter long ''scrolls'' of double-strength soft white tissue can help at other occasions of catharsis.

Why Sleep in Public?

One might be excused for thinking that the men in suits sleeping near the station are simply the victims of blind inebriety. Nothing is that simple, however.

A careful examination of the prostrate forms will show that many are still attached to umbrellas and brown envelopes and therefore normal *salarymen*, with wives waiting at home or company dormitories at the end of the Chuo Line. So why are they sleeping here? One answer is Nostalgia. The general state of well-being induced by formidable quantities of draft beer and whiskey stimulates the desire to return to the comforts of the past — for example, the stiff bean-bag pillow and hard mattress of a misspent childhood in the mountains of Yamagata, or that first night under the stars in a fishingboat somewhere off Shikoku. Not the decadent luxury of the soft semi-double bed with pink sheets that should lure them home now. Hence the attraction of the concrete with the distant background wash of the last train announcement.

Add to this state answer No. 2. This is Masochism, encouraged by TV programs of "The Challenger" variety, much-loved around the world for their sense of Oriental lunacy. In summer, the game is "Mosquito Macho," the voluntary sacrifice of one's body on a station bench. The challenge for the mosquito is to pierce not only the cheap Daiei suit but also the long underwear. In winter, the game is "Frostbite Fever." The challenge for the cold is to penetrate the heatlayer resulting from several liters of hot

sake.

Add to these answer No. 3, particularly in the case of the rather clean *salaryman.* This is known as "Post-Soap Syndrome" and is roughly akin to the Western "Lipstick-on-the-Collar Condition." It is widespread.

It works like this. Hubby leaves home at 6:30 a.m., barely recovered from the carousing of the previous night. He has slept for four hours and spoken three words to his children, even less to his wife. There has been no physical contact, at least as far as he is aware. Twelve hours later he leaves work and drinks for the next four hours. He is now showing predictable signs of wear and tear. At this point the animal spirit arises within him and he seeks solace in the sudsy arms and charms of a willing college girl earning much more per hour than he ever will. Ninety minutes and 1 ½ times later, he emerges a new man, invigorated, comfortable, smiling . . . and clean! This will never do. He has just done exactly what his wife suspects he is doing. His long day's night is far from being over. He moves into

Remedial Mode. To destroy any lingering fragrance he needs a bowl of *ramen*, a plate of *gyoza* and a glass of straight *shochu*. To destroy the cleanliness, what better, easier and more convincing way than curling up in front of the station, or on a nice hard bench if he can locate one?

A scrubbed and sober *salaryman* arriving home at 1:30 a.m. is not only a contradiction in terms, it is a personal disgrace.

Why Do It in the Street?

Nobody likes to act just like his own national stereotype: there are plenty of Englishmen who are definitely not gentlemen, some Frenchmen must be suspected of going out of their way not to be good lovers, and how many Russians have you met who really did have snow on their boots? In the same way, when a Japanese man hears of his national reputation for cleanliness and politeness, it is only natural for him to rebel against it, and show the world how he is not going to be tied down by role models not of his own making. And what better way to express one's contempt for all this than to unzip and spray the neighbor's gatepost?

In fact, there is an element of schizophrenia, for if you observe these peers closely, they tend to choose locations which are easily visible to the public; in other words, they don't go behind trees or in especially dark corners like the English so-called gentleman would, but stand clearly illuminated or silhouetted in that unmistakable pose for all to see. And yet they do not face their audience. How is this schizophrenic display of the performance but concealment of the equipment to be interpreted? Further research is urgently required.

Some may say that any right-minded man would rather "go" outside than in one of those evil-smelling public toilets to be found in stations. But this is false reasoning. The foul smell in fact proves that many men do choose to visit those places. But sometimes there is no choice. For many years Japan was well known for its lack of public conveniences: there was no choice but to do it in the street. Now, although many local authorities have erected public *benjos,* many men are conditioned to believe that there are none. Hence the sight of whole coachloads urinating against the outside wall of the toilet at an expressway rest area. And remember that many men are caught with the urge late in the evening, after a few drinks, at a time when the department stores, which their wives use freely when caught in similar circumstances of distress, are closed.

Then, of course, there is our old friend communication with nature. The days are still easily within living memory when Seibu Line trains used to carry loads of night soil out to the agricultural areas of Nerima and beyond, and the agricultural spirit still flows in the blood even of *Homo salarymanensis.* So recycle the stuff directly, without even buying a railway ticket for it, and let the cool night air caress your most valued possessions. What's that? Your agricultural spirit tells you that urine doesn't help concrete walls to grow? Well, too late now. You can't stop in midstream.

Why Not on the Floor?

Have you noticed? A lot of Japanese people are extremely reluctant to put shopping bags, briefcases, even suitcases down on the ground, or on the floor in trains, etc. Well, if you had just spent a six-figure sum on imitation alligator luggage or golfing bags, you wouldn't want to put them down somewhere where others have deposited their spit and, who knows, other bodily fluids, would you?

That explains why even the nicest, gentlest-looking old lady — correction, especially the nicest, gentlest-looking old lady — will fight for a seat on the train, only to put her bags down on it and remain standing herself. Or, if she finds more than one seat she will sit down and surround herself with a fortress of baggage. She can't reach the luggage rack, but she will not put her things on the floor. After all, if you put a bag on the floor, that means it has gone where shoes go, and so you'll have to leave it at the door, too, when you get home. And that can be very inconvenient.

Perhaps this also explains why schoolchildren are forced, as part of their compulsory uniform, to shoulder heavy satchels to and from school every day: hanging the bags from their shoulders is the surest way of ensuring that they don't, even for one moment, let the bag come into contact with, horror of horrors, the ground.

So the thinking seems to go not this way: "The street is a place where we might need to put our bags down, so let's keep it clean," but: "We can't expect the street to be clean, so let's avoid putting our bags down on it." Which may appear to be defeatist, but if you think about it it's pragmatic, and far more realistic. When did you last lean your briefcase against a lamppost in any country secure in the knowledge that the few square feet around that lamppost were spick and span to the point of sterility?

Why Bicycles and Umbrellas?

Each society has its own feelings about what is common property. In an extreme case, like Saudi Arabia, the general feeling is that everything within the country is to be shared among friends. In such a situation, one borrows, one doesn't "steal." And certainly nobody is going to accuse an acquaintance of stealing when the punishment could be a sudden and permanent loss of use of the hand.

Japan is much more oriented towards private ownership, except when it comes to umbrellas and bicycles. Now, this is really a rather interesting phenomenon. Japanese houses and shops have a tendency to spill over into the street and one problem foreigners face is making a distinction between genuine *gomi* and house overflow. Japanese seem to know instinctively which is which. They know that the 23-inch" TV in perfect working order by the lamppost is up for grabs, whereas the attractive *bonsai/hibachi* set one meter away is private property. How this is proved never seems very clear.

But when we come to umbrellas and bicycles, everything changes. Suddenly it is a case of "What is yours is mine," and even the police, who will at least attempt to find properly documented bicycles, clearly do not regard this particular form of acquirement as a very heinous crime.

Perhaps we should separate the two crimes. Many Japanese umbrellas it is true, are cheap, do get left a lot on trains, and are even provided by some charitable shops for their customers. And most Japanese seem to think that "borrowing" an umbrella in time of need is quite normal and is indeed a kind of give-and-take situation. However, actual experience shows that it is often the expensive umbrella which is taken. This suggests that the need is not restricted to a quick covering in time of rain.

In fact, the Japanese are undoubtedly a nation of umbrella kleptomaniacs, however low the crime rate may be. Many foreigners soon discover this and find themselves joining in the general game. Ask any foreigner how many of his umbrellas he actually bought and legally owns. The justification seems to be that if everyone does it, it can't be all that bad. The same argument is also used by cannibals.

Bicycles are a much more serious problem involving bigger money. And once again, as any desperate owner of his fifth bicycle in two years will tell you, although there are clearly cases of old, unlocked bicycles being "borrowed" to speed up the journey home from the station, it is the expensive, foreign-made bicycles that mostly get stolen, and in huge numbers.

Locks are no deterrent: there are cases of triple-locked bikes being sawn away from their moorings. The police tend to dismiss such incidents as a game played by boys who need to brighten up a dull *manga*-filled adolescence.

Insurance companies hesitate to oblige "because bicycles get stolen." So you can fix your 10-speed, ¥80,000 dream with superglue to the station railings and find it mysteriously gone an hour later, report it and be shrugged off with obvious disinterest. On the other hand, you can have an amateur *ninja* in through your window, take ¥150 out of your telephone piggy bank, and then be besieged by the forensic men and the Japanese version of Inspector Poirot.

But perhaps we should be grateful that kleptomania is restricted to these two humble items of everyday life. No society is perfect, and if the natural urge to "borrow" is thus assuaged, then better to smile wryly, get wet and walk home.

Why Not Smile?

When photography was introduced to Japan in the Meiji Period, Westerners didn't smile for photos, either. With such long exposure times required, they had to assume poses that could be held steady for several seconds. This is difficult with a smile, which has to be spontaneous. But the Japanese must have misinterpreted it as a Western tradition to be adopted and copied for the sake of appearing civilized and enlightened.

Since those early days, photography has advanced, due to a great extent to Japanese research and skill. Stiff, wooden poses are no longer required — at least not for technical purposes. But they have become ingrained in

Japanese tradition and culture, so that a man who has just won a figure followed by several zeroes in a lottery can be photographed poker-faced, indeed morose and surly-looking. Parents who have found their children lost in China decades ago appear in photos as if they'd just been sentenced to 15 years' hard labor.

On the other hand, an action shot of someone falling off a bicycle into the path of an oncoming bus will show the victim smiling. A smile will be plastered across the face of a bank clerk who has just handed over even more zeroes to a bank robber carrying a water pistol. And that's the point: a smile in Japan indicates acute embarrassment, not relaxed goodwill in front of a camera. Watch next time you're at a station. Who smiles most broadly, the person who just squeaks on to the train before the doors close, or the one who just misses it, but sees his briefcase disappearing down the track trapped in the doors?

Then take a trip some time to the double bridge in front of the Imperial Palace, Disneyland, a famous waterfall, or any of those places where there are benches for large group photographs. Watch the group line up smiling and giggling, and then watch how they all turn their merry smiles to scowling grimaces when the photographer tells them he is ready. Flash! — and there is a record of what you might think was the most boring day ever spent at the seaside, circus, zoo or whatever.

But then watch the faces wreathe themselves again in smiles once the session is over. And look how the sun glints on those teeth, or rather on those missing parts of teeth replaced by gold or other precious metals. Aha! Is that perhaps the reason smiling is not done? Would the glint of a filling reflect too much of the camera's flash, and turn the whole picture to a brilliant white blur?

The frown, which began as a necessity on account of early primitive equipment, is now just as necessary, but is due to the sophistication of modern equipment. The more things change, the more they stay the same.

Why Group Travel?

The lone American tourist in, say, Paris asks this question in desperation while attempting to struggle through the serried ranks of a Japanese package group as they follow their tour leader's flag round the Louvre. The Parisian hotelier asks the same question in bemused delight a few hours later as the same package group descends on his hotel and, for a moment free of the leader's hypnotic flag, goes berserk in a wild extravaganza of spending. Within minutes the shelves of the hotel's shop have been stripped of knitwear, porcelain, leather and assorted handicrafts, and the bar has run dry of its most expensive brandies, its champagnes and its small stock of Japanese beer.

So there's the answer: it's good for business. You might think that after 250 years of enforced isolation in the Edo Period, the Japanese would be straining at the leash to go abroad. Or even go anywhere, as in Edo Japan nobody below samurai was permitted to go anywhere at all except on foot, and that at great expense. But not so. Many accept the acknowledged fact that Japan is geographically too far

from the touristy lands like Switzerland or the centers of
modern "civilization" like Los Angeles. So they're happy
to stay at home. And when at home, if you have to stand
on trains for up to four hours a day just to get to and from
work, who's interested in traveling during those precious
few vacations?

But it's good for business, so out come the public relations boys and by sheer commercial overkill they manage
to persuade normally rational people that the ultimate in
unique fashion de luxe is to fly to Hawaii with a jumbo-
load of other unique-experience-seekers, there to stay for
half the price of a normal air fare in a hotel identical to the
one run by the same department-store company in front of
the station at home. And the same commercial message
works at home, so that coachloads from Yokohama take off
for a few days in Kobe; hordes from the slopes of Fuji have
a weekend on Mount Aso; parties from Kanazawa visit the
gardens at Mito. In other words, tens of thousands of yen
(often more than for a trip to Hong Kong or Singapore) are
spent on traveling hundreds of miles to see a place just like
home.

Why? you ask in desperation or delight, depending on
position vis-à-vis these groups. How can the tour operators
get away with it? The answer is that flag: if a crowd from
Nagoya going round Osaka Castle keeps its eyes on the
flag, no one will notice that there's hardly any difference
between where they are and home. And another thing.
You try walking into a London hotel alone and asking for
misoshiru. No go. But try in a group of 50 or so, with a promise of more groups to come, and *misoshiru* will be forth-

coming before you can say *itadakimasu*. To the average Japanese traveler abroad who needs *misoshiru* like a koala needs eucalyptus leaves, this is a big consideration, and will send even the fiercest individualist scurrying to join the flock.

VII
Traffic and Transportation

Why LHD Jaguars?

This is a wonderful instance of international harmony — the harmony between silly Japanese ostentation and inept British export marketing.

The British, being an island nation, tend to think of themselves as unique. They automatically, but wrongly, assume that their customs and traditions are restricted to their own shores and that all foreigners (who begin at Calais) do everything the wrong way round. One of their customs is driving on the left, and therefore having right-hand-drive cars. The Brits think they are the only ones in the universe who drive on the left, while all foreigners, whether as near as Calais and Ostend or as far away as Tokyo and Yokohama, drive on the wrong side of the road, i.e., the right.

Don't blame them too strongly for this: for a country with very little of its car export business left, it doesn't really matter what silly notions they entertain. Except with luxury cars. For the export business for luxury cars still thrives, with thousands of Jaguars, Rolls-Royces and so on being shipped annually to such wrong-side-of-the-road places as the U.S., West Germany and the Middle East. So perhaps it's not altogether surprising that Jaguar salesmen appear to be convinced that Japan, too, drives on the right and needs left-hand-drive cars.

But as everyone knows, Japan drives on the left, just like Britain — thus deflating simultaneously both Japanese and British myths about respective uniqueness. So you might expect cars made for driving on the right not to sell so well. Far from it. Jaguar trade figures are kept healthy by swanky dentists who have nothing better to do with their money than throw it away on expensive foreign cars capable of speeds many times higher than any speed that could possibly be attained on any road in Japan. And just to underline and overdo the ostentation, they like them left-hand-drive, so that everyone can see at a glance how different they are — or at least how different they are from everybody except all the other dentists in LHD Jaguars, lawyers in LHD Mercedes, architects in LHD Volkswagens (usually yellow), gangsters in LHD Cadillacs, and rich layabouts in LHD BMWs. Perhaps you can't blame the gangsters: Cadillacs with the steering wheel on the right are not available, are they?

Another point has to do with the trick of parallel importing. If you're rich and innocent you go to the foreign car company's main agent in Japan, which just happens to be the same company for just about whatever foreign car you want. With its virtual monopoly this company can get away with charging sums that even dentists or politicians might wonder at. But if you have a little bit of sense (which we hope goes with being a dentist) you go to a minor agent who gets his cars by a more roundabout route but still charges less for them. Some of them have been redirected from other destinations where they drive on the right, and so, by paying less you actually get the added bonus of a prestigious LHD car, which jealous Cherry or Cedric drivers have to look twice at before they can see the driver. And when you park your car illegally in the street in front of your office, mistress' apartment or *pachinko* parlor, you can open the door and walk straight in without being seen.

Why on the Left?

The Japanese drive on the left because the steering wheel's on the right. Okay, okay, so now you're going to ask why the steering wheel's on the right. That's easy: it's an economy measure at the car manufacturing plants. In the old days, when steering wheels were installed by living human beings, one man stood between two production lines, and fixed one in on the nearest side of each car that came to him. In this way, a car that approached him on his right got one on its right, and went for domestic sales; one that approached him on his left became left-hand-drive, and went for export.

But sooner or later they needed more and more for export, and couldn't find enough skilled left-handed car workers. They tried turning the workers round, but then they couldn't see the cars coming, which slowed them down at least a second per car. Now it's all done by robots which can be made more or less left-handed as export demand rises or falls.

Perhaps that still doesn't really explain why they drove on the left to begin with. In a word, it was in order to be unique. Watch the look of disappointment when you point out that they drive on the left in the U.K., too, and Australia, and New Zealand, and India, and half of Africa. . . .

Then there are the historical origins, which go way back beyond the postwar years when British cars were manufactured in Japan under license, and even beyond 1872, when Japan's first railway, built with British technical advice, started its trains running on the left. In fact, they go right back to those good old founders of so many quaint traditions (like testing a new sword by seeing how many convicts' bodies it could cut through in one go), the samurai.

As they wore their swords on their left, they always walked on the left, to avoid getting their swords accidentally tangled up when they passed, and also of course so that they could easily draw their swords with their right hands (left-handed samurai were as rare as left-handed autoworkers), and effortlessly hack to death an approaching enemy.

Why on the Wrong Side?

Japan is a cyclist's paradise. The cyclist, whether policeman or postman, schoolgirl or *sushi* delivery man, priest or paperboy, has carte blanche to pedal anywhere — on or off the road, or in any direction. This right of passage derives from the transition point between horse and *jinrikisha*. What is a bicycle, after all, but a fast-moving pedestrian? And Japanese pedestrians take great delight in walking in the middle of the road, even when there is a sidewalk provided. A horse was also a fast-moving pedestrian and a rickshaw was two or more fast-moving pedestrians.

The assumption is, of course, that drivers and pedestrians alike will respect the freedom of the cyclist, and most of the time they do. After all, it could be your granny on the bicycle, or your wife with kids at both ends. Blatant refusal to recognize the concept of a one-way street ties in with the death wish, however. It is on a par with those semi-professional cyclists who desperately want to upgrade their status by taking on the trucks even when a special bicycle-lane is provided. That is, however, a universal phenomenon.

But the idea of riding your full-size adult bike along the sidewalk, across pedestrian crossings, and anywhere else negotiable, is a wonderful example of the Japanese belief in equality and freedom of the individual. It had to be that way, anyway, because most roads are not wide enough to support a real bicycle lane. The compromise solution is to mark out a lane on the sidewalk, but not make it exclusive. Everyone can gain by it if they want to, so nobody ever

argues with cyclists.

There is, however, one gray area when it comes to defining what is or is not a bicycle. This is the recent growing popularity of the unicycle, perhaps the safest and handiest mode of transport known to Man after feet. By definition a unicycle is not a bicycle, but it resembles one. Unicyclists will of course claim to be simple fast-moving pedestrians because they can stop or turn on the spot just like you or me. This is a big problem for Railway officials in particular. Unicyclists have been known to cycle through the turnstiles of Shinjuku Station, along the platform and even down the steps. (They can rarely be seen going up the steps.) This is apparently not dangerous and takes up no more room than an awkward, two-legged slow-moving pedestrian. In other words, give a bicyclist freedom and you must give a unicyclist even more freedom. Better still, encourage everyone to become a unicyclist. Then people could move around faster and there would be no need to park outside the station either, because you can fold the thing up and carry it round with you.

A final point: a bicycle without a person attached becomes instant public property to be stolen, kicked, knocked over and generally abused. And a motorbike, particularly with a person attached, is a completely different story — ask any truckdriver.

Why Lost Taxis?

You would expect taxi-drivers in Japan to know the way. It is a very well-known fact in Japan that the streets of London are crammed with would-be taxi-drivers desperately racing around the city on bicycles or mopeds trying to remember every landmark, street name and shortcut. Only with that information firmly tucked away in his head can the aspirant ever hope to rise to the exalted rank of "cabbie," a much-respected and much-tipped personage.

Another well-known fact is that many Japanese city taxi-drivers have not the slightest idea where they are, where you want them to go, or how to get there. Why is this? Isn't there a test for Japanese taxi-drivers? No. They just have to be able to drive, preferably dangerously. But why does this situation exist?

First, we must look at the status of the taxi in Japan. It is a basic part of life for perhaps a majority of people, not because it is a cheap means of transport (it isn't) but because there are so many taxis available and they do help one to avoid the hustle and bustle of crowded trains and buses. But there is no real excitement involved in getting into a taxi in Japan, no prestige, nothing special about the vehicle itself. And, as for the status of the driver himself, it is a job which seems to involve little self-pride. There are, of course, the dedicated professionals in white gloves and caps, the ones who insist on driving 1963 Toyotas, and the ones with *karaoke,* massage and TV, but clearly it is not an honorable profession to the majority.

The problem lies with those who become taxi-drivers: lots of failed jazz musicians, bankers, television directors, palanquin-bearers and the like. After all, what real advantages are there in being a daytime driver stuck in a jam or an all-nighter with a drunken slob in the back seat? There are only two advantages: the chances for conversation (English practice or industrial espionage) and the thrill of ignoring potential customers on a wet night in Roppongi.

There is not much incentive, either, for providing good service in order to get a decent tip. Most customers insist on having their change and know that the driver is expected to run after them with the change if they forget. Not much joy there. And the only drivers who feel entitled to charge for luggage carried are those who carry skis on the roof. That is why the others will grumble as they shuffle to the trunk to move the towels off the clothesline and shift the golf clubs out of the way in an attempt to fit in a single suitcase. No joy there, either.

Having suggested that there is a certain lack of job pride involved, we now come to the main answer to the question: most taxi-drivers arrived in the big city yesterday and genuinely have not a clue where Roppongi is (although they've seen the discos on TV), let alone "Almond" coffee shop. This is especially true of truly cosmopolitan Tokyo, that melting pot of yokels from Yamagata and Yamaguchi with ne'er an *Edokko* in sight.

But do the customers complain? Rarely. You see, most of them are country types too, glad to chat nostalgically about the glories of life in the rice paddies, glad to help out. Everyone has a first day in the city.

Why Salute Trains?

Why does anyone salute anything, or anybody (which is more normal)? Let us look at an Oxford English Dictionary definition of salute (n.):

"gesture expressing respect, homage or courteous recognition, to person especially when arriving or departing."

If you were in Britain, you might expect military persons, policemen, bus drivers, driving school instructors and Boy Scouts to salute each other. If you were in the USA you would expect the President to do it every 30 seconds. But you would not expect station managers or their deputies to salute trains, even though British Rail employees have been seen waving flags and lanterns as trains depart.

So how has this interesting phenomenon developed of men in white gloves saluting disappearing trains, whether or not they stopped at the station, and indeed with even greater respect when it is an express train passing through at high speed?

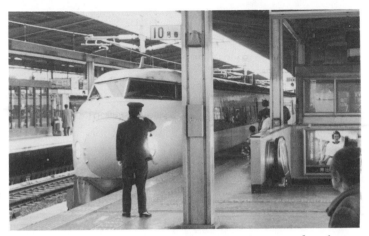

If it is a "gesture expressing respect," we need to know to what or to whom the respect is being shown. It might be respect for the train guard (conductor) who has the onerous job of being responsible for the welfare of his passengers, certainly more conscientiously so than his British counterparts. On the other hand, it could be respect for the train itself. Respect for a train? Well, that makes a kind of sense: without the train there would be no job, and saluting a train is more fun than saluting a bulldozer.

If it is "homage," then we are talking about dutiful reverence, acknowledgment of superiority or formal public acknowledgment of allegiance. So it could mean that the saluting official is simultaneously showing his feelings towards the Railwaymen's Union while letting the passing guard feel superior.

"Courteous recognition" clearly means that he wants no one to forget that this is a train, not a bird, not a plane and only slightly inferior to Superman.

"To person. . . ." definitely rules out the train itself. However, if one looks carefully, there is not always any sign of recognition from the guard who is being treated with respect. Perhaps he really is superior?

The conclusion of all this is far from conclusive, but we are clearly involved with an obscure part of the Japanese Natural Respect (JNR for short, or just JR for even shorter). It perhaps works something like this: the train itself, the driver and the guard are a unit, but they are also part of a great debt-ridden system which includes everyone from the humble part-time clippie to the poor devil who stands on the platform ready to drag people off the tracks and recover small girls' hats with a pair of super-pincers. The salute recognizes the oneness of it all. It is celebration of the fact that the trains are still running, that all of us still have work and that nobody jumped in front of this particular train. It is something to do on a cold morning. It is a vain attempt to be noticed. It is a sign of relief that the train has now moved on and become someone else's responsibility.

Why Leave *Manga?*

If you open one, you should have a good idea why people leave behind the comic books they have been reading on the train. Would you bring such scenes of blood and gore, sex and warped fantasy into your home? Popped eyeballs and blank crotches aside (pubic hair cannot be legally published in Japan), the quality of paper and printing suggest they are better thrown away. Most are brittle, brown, rough newsprint stock printed in three colors — one color at a time, that is — all smudged and flecked with bare spots like confetti. On second thought, the question better seems to be why read one in the first place?

The average reader falls into two categories: bona fide adolescents of both sexes for whom many *manga* profess to be written, and adult males who comprise a special market. Analogous fare written for adult females is usually published as inserts in more expensive magazines, which are seldom left behind on trains. Adolescents don't leave them behind unless they already have the same one or have torn out the part they want. Girls, especially, trade theirs with their friends.

The ones who leave them on the train are the middle executives or their subalterns. Top executives don't ride trains, so it is not clear whether they read comics or not . . . they could be just as shocked as you with modern fare.

One important reason for leaving them on the train is the sheer quantity of them. Most titles are published weekly. The thickest ones contain several serialized stories cranked out by teams of writers and artists just ahead of their deadline to be rushed into print and distributed at the entrances of most train stations throughout Japan. This blanket distribution is possible since the largest publishers in Japan produce these right alongside some of the most sophisticated scholarly tomes in existence. There is no difficulty in finding new ones for each day of the week.

At or near 200 yen per copy, the cost is far less than the usual train fare. Further, since most commuters' fares are paid by their employers, it represents the only cost for the trip. Along with an even cheaper daily tabloid, the comic *magajiin* will be devoured within the course of the two-hour commute that the average reader must suffer daily.

Ordinarily, the pages are flipped almost as fast as the old Kinetoscope photos with scenes about as amusing or titillating as that of penny-arcade slapstick. Except in times when recycled paper is high-priced and a few volumes can be exchanged for a roll of toilet paper, the majority will be flipped up on to the luggage rack as Ichiro or Saburo races to avoid missing his stop. When recyclable paper prices are low, no one has shelf space for the occasional classic that may be worth keeping since they will most certainly be anthologized in reduced size on higher-quality paper.

The only collectors are a few of the unemployed who have fallen through the safety net (and statistics, as well) for the unemployed. Instead of trading for toilet paper, they avoid the middleman altogether and exchange them for enough cash for a little red-eye (sold appropriately as "Red Label"). Also, a few tall foreigners have been observed following Ichiro or Saburo and furtively picking up some free texts for studying Japanese language or culture or . . . NihONSENSE.

Why Spread Legs?

Japanese men who spread their legs out when they get a seat on the train are creating the modern Japanese legend of overcrowded trains. If they all put their legs together, there would be room for many more to sit down; then the train wouldn't be so crowded with standing passengers, and Japan would lose one of its most cherished international reputations. The leg-spreaders, at the cost of considerable discomfort to themselves (you try standing up and walking normally after you've had your legs at 135° for an hour or so) are helping their country to hold its head high in the international community.

Others reject this argument and claim it's a result of the bone formation being affected by spending the first months of life strapped to the back of one's mother or grandmother or sister or any other convenient woman, and then later sitting cross-legged on the floor. This matter is dealt with elsewhere, but here suffice it to say that this argument has as many holes in it as one of those special plastic bags you can get for keeping in the sink and throwing kitchen refuse away in. After all, baby girls are carried on backs, too, and women who spread their legs out on trains are very rare (even when they are sitting down and not forced by their husbands to stand, precariously balanced by a baby on the back and shopping bags in the front, while the husband occupies room for three with his legs spread out east-south-east and west-south-west). Also, sitting on the floor is becoming less and less common. Most homes now have tables, and we don't know of a single office where the *salarymen* sit cross-legged at low desks.

So it's a bit more likely that this phenomenon represents something psychological rather than physiological: it is a yearning for the safety of *o-kaasan's* back, or a yearning for the simple days of yore when you didn't have to spend all your money on nasty Western things like tables, or all your time in a boring office, but could plant yourself *daimyo*-like on a soft cushion on the *tatami,* and just wait to be waited upon by all and sundry.

Rumors that leg-spreading is the result of an epidemic of elephantiasis of the genitals caused by a virus in train seats should be ignored. They do explain why more modest men prefer to stand, but we believe they were started maliciously by some jealous, underendowed person.

On the other hand, there are some who claim that those who spread their legs can do so with impunity because they themselves are underendowed and run no risk of accidental exposure, no matter how openly they display their um, er, um, er, um. This claim must surely be one of sour grapes.

Why Let Kids Sit?

The reason children always get to sit down on trains is training. It all boils down to training.

In a recent British TV interview, the Japanese-born British author Kazuo Ishiguro said that he is still horrified at the way British parents treat their children — stopping them in the middle of a game, for example, in order to send them on an errand. Such lack of indulgence he finds extraordinary.

The point is that the Japanese child is treated in a way very different from its counterbrats elsewhere. It is allowed to dangle sloppily from its mother's back; it is given the dubious pleasure of having its mother lie down to sleep with it; it is allowed to shout, scream and cavort; and it is allowed to take up valuable seating space on trains and buses while inferior adults, war-wounded and cripples have to stand.

The message seems to be very clear: never mind about granny, let the poor kids have a good time while they can. And that is the main reason for this social perversion. All the parents and doting grandparents involved in this coddling scam know very well that once the child reaches the age of reason (this varies, but in most cases comes soon enough, in others never) it will have all the pleasure knocked out of it in favor of rip-off *juku* operators.

In one way, letting children sit down, particularly on rickety old buses, makes some sense as there really is very little for children to hold on to. It is not uncommon to see groups of standing schoolchildren desperately hanging on to each other as they sway en masse. But lack of discipline at this stage means that many of the kids who are always allowed a seat will continue the selfish habit into early adulthood and beyond. The weak shall stand, and the strong will inherit the seat.

There are, of course, ways of taking the seat into your own hands. If you happen to be Japanese, you are expected to smile indulgently at the kids sprawled out along the seat and remember happier days when you too did the same thing. If you happen to be non-Japanese, and particularly a red-faced and rather large *hakujin*, you are expected to do the same. However, the hackles tend to rise within any well-trained British person, as memories flood back of all those times you were forced to stand in favor of the respected aged or the deserving female of the species. The child on the seat is already slightly perturbed at the sight of the red face before it, so now is the time to move in for the kill. There is no better way to shock a Japanese child than to lift it bodily from the seat and plonk it in front of its open-mouthed mother.

This action does little to improve international harmony, but it is certain that without such discipline from an early age the young hopeful will grow up with weak legs, a tendency to sit spread-eagled and without that respect for the aged which is always stated as a strong characteristic of Japanese society.

Having said all that, there is the even more disturbing sight of nasty foreign superbrats taking advantage of the situation and making a terrible noise into the bargain. The best solution for that is to detrain oneself as soon as possible and change cars.

And if we really are forced to stand, well, a little self-discipline never did any harm, did it?

Why on the Back?

Why do Japanese mothers carry their babies on their backs? First of all, it's not only mothers. In the extended families that are not as common as they used to be, but still do exist, strapping the baby to its grandmother's back is a good way of keeping both Baby and Grandma out of trouble. If Grandma really is as young as she looks, then she needs to be kept out of trouble, and the same can be said, in mirror image as it were, for the reason why Baby is so

often strapped to Big Sister's back. If she's as old as she looks (which she probably isn't — postwar prosperity has done wonders for the physical development of teenagers) she will need to be restricted in some way, and a baby on your back is probably better than being chained like a dog, if only by a fraction.

Children in Japan are a burden. From when they reach school age, or rather kindergarten age, to when they finish their education (nowadays not uncommonly the mid-twenties) they devour everything: all the food in the refrigerator; all the space in the house for their studydesks and video games; and any money that's left for private school fees, *juku* fees, driving school fees, and fares for skiing trips to the Japan Alps.

It is their mothers who support all this and force the fathers to spend 15 hours a day at work trying to scrape up enough money to afford this massive expense. And why are the mothers so enthusiastic? Because they are so pleased to have the little brats literally off their backs, where they've been for the first three years of their lives, that they will do anything for their offspring. To the mother, the financial burden is as light as a feather compared with the burden of a budding sumo wrestler on your back, crying and burping directly into your ear and pulling your hair in a misguided display of filial piety.

Filial piety is important in Japanese society, and so, they say, is something called "skinship." Although it sounds as if it does, this really has nothing to do with contraceptive devices; it refers to the close human-body-to-human-body contact that is part and parcel of living in a small country like Japan. In Japanese society, people eat, work, live, and especially travel closer to each other than in any other "advanced" nation. The skinship that is forced upon them every morning in a commuter train is so close as to go beyond embarrassment; the same can be said of department stores on the day their baseball team has won a championship or the mountain lodges at each stage up Mount Fuji. Patience in extreme cases of involuntary skinship has to be trained from an early age, and after all where better than your mother's back to learn to be half-smothered but still not to kick, faint, be sick or wet yourself?

The theory that being carried on your mother's back makes it easier for you to sit on *tatami* later in life is discussed elsewhere; the spirit of self-sacrifice with which mothers deliberately mutilate their own figures by crossing those straps across their breasts is too heroic a matter to discuss in these humble pages.

Why Not Motels?

When there are so many motels all over Japan, why do you never see families staying in them?

Well, for openers, most families expect mirrors on the wall, not over the bed! It seems that the Japanese hostelry industry conceived of the motel in postwar times when cars were first available to the masses. Thus motels are only an adjunct to pre-existing alternatives. The upshot is that what American motels can only see as the frosting on the cake, the Japanese have developed as a mainstay.

For example, a few U.S. motel managers accept gratuities in return for the use of unmade-up rooms early in the day for lunchtime ''quickies'' by patrons of their attached restaurant. They could hardly sustain their enterprise on such business alone, even at all-night rates. The era of free sex creates little demand for rental facilities. In Japan, however, even paid sex requires additional rental facilities, often at an hourly rate. (We haven't determined, however, if prostitutes get a kickback or not from regular usage — in most countries they must pay a kickback, but Japan is not most countries. . , .)

With names like ''Sweet Cherry'' or ''Peach'' (*momo* in Japanese — a synonym for thighs or ''butt''), motels have lurid signs in lilac and yellow or rose, white and navy blue jarring night skies in the peaceful countryside. They're stuck on any road remotely connected, coming and going: "You have just missed Paradise Spot Motel 2 kilometers back and left 500 meters." Left? facing which way?

OK, then what *do* families do — sleep in the car? Normal families have few chances to travel, usually only during times when everyone and their kid brother are on the road. Indeed, they have on occasion had to sleep in the car. But due to traffic conditions only: they simply couldn't reach their destination where they had a reservation often as much as a year in advance. Further, families with school-age children have few outings together since school trips or events are scheduled even on such universal holidays as New Year's Day— swimming team trials, ski trips, special examinations, etc.

Travel is more often by train, bus or plane than by car (the cost break is at about 2½ persons before auto travel is cheaper, on average, not to mention the opportunity to rest on overnight mass transportation facilities).

Lodging can be had at the very cheap low-cost youth hostels (not limited to youth — favored by cyclists) at hot springs, ski facilities, the seaside or even in the wilderness. For the impoverished or stingy who actually enjoy home-cooked instant *misoshiru* for breakfast, there are low-cost *minshuku* ("people's accommodation"). Those who prefer to imagine that a little more expertise and lavish care has gone into dishing up their early morning raw egg can book in at high-cost *ryokan* (travelers' inns), that provide traditional-style lodging for a night or a week. The *ryokan* strive for aeshetic effects and service while *minshuku* are more basic. Even more popular, recently, are second homes and company-owned lodges that can be rented at reasonable, even bargain prices near popular resort areas.

Most of these options are as convenient, or more so, than any Western-style motel. In short, only trysters with something to hide really need a motel.

VIII
Environs and Environment

Why *Onsen?*

Hot-spring baths, or *onsen,* abound in this volcanic land. Old-age pensioners' bus tours, businessmen's "business" trips, students' "study" circles converge on them in their thousands, to wallow in the life-giving 44° waters and get drunk afterwards on cheap 43° whiskey. If they do it in that order, there are few casualties, but unfortunately there are the ignorant innocents who try it the other way round, in which case the waters turn out to be life-taking rather than giving.

They say that before the Allies appeared on the scene the sexes bathed innocently together, although it's hard to see what is so innocent about that. Then, in response to the castigations of high-minded, low-spirited missionaries, the first gesture was to divide public bathing places . . . with a rope! Now, alas, there is total segregation, with just two exceptions: the person at the entrance counter of a public bathhouse can see in both sides, and some *onsen* are still mixed. So any *gaijin* who wants a peek at, er, well, you know, should try to find one of these remote *onsen* — employment as public bath counter clerk not being covered by most working visas.

The Japanese people, of course, enjoy *onsen* not for this shockingly lewd, rude reason, but in order to return to that age of innocence that was so utterly destroyed when Western influence invaded and corrupted the people just as the snake in the garden of Eden did to Eve. They go to find peace and tranquility — not lewdness and licentiousness, but liberty from all the taboos and regulations that oppress and restrain modern Japanese society. The hot, sulfurous waters soothe the body and refresh the soul, providing relief from the stresses and strains of modern ''civilized'' life. While thus involved in a process of self-purification, who could be so base as to consider such mundane matters as the sight of naked bodies of the opposite sex?

In any case, with all that steam swirling about and the bath itself bubbling and churning with volcanic spring water, you can't see your own body, let alone that of anyone else. The stink of the sulfur is hardly conducive to ribald thoughts, either. But the Japanese know that, surrounded by those bubbles, steam and stink, they can flout one of society's strictest taboos. They can fart to their hearts' content, and nobody will notice.

Why at Scenic Spots?

The reason people dump electric appliances at scenic spots is similar to the reason why dogs pee on poles and snails leave glistening tracks: to show that they've been there, and anyone who comes afterwards is not the first to lay claim to the territory.

There are those who claim that this is a filthy, inexcusable habit in a nation that prides itself with a long, long tradition of affinity with nature, but they don't see the point. After all, old fridges, sewing machines and rotten bedding are only thrown *down* ravines and valleys, so that as long as you look *up,* you can still enjoy a distant view of (apparently) unsullied mountains. Those dull, introverted souls who insist on casting their eyes downwards to where your old washing machine lies tangled in the weeds have only themselves to blame for not widening their horizons. And anyway, in modern, hectic Japan there is little time for the ordinary city-dweller to enjoy the countryside, so what better way than to pension off a treasured family possession, such as a clapped out old TV, to enjoy some rural serenity by proxy over the years?

In fact, chucking everything from cigarette butts to wardrobes out of car windows is one of the most public-spirited things a citizen of Japan can do, and for several reasons.

One is that clearing all the trash up once a year gives much-needed employment to local depressed agricultural workers, and provides encouragement for voluntary groups such as Scouts, Lions and neighborhood associations to do their bit for beautification of the environment and maybe even make a bit of money off the scrap dealer.

Another is that everybody knows the city trash-collecting systems are already overloaded; a bit of independent, do-it-yourself garbage disposal will lighten the burden on city dumps.

Furthermore, this can be seen as a gesture of sympathy for electrical appliance dealers. Of course, every dealer will offer to take away your old oven-toaster when you buy a new electronic oven that will magic up roast beef in three minutes and tell you in a computerized voice when it's ready, but if you were to accept the dealer's kind offer, that would impose on you some kind of *giri* and make you indebted to him. Not only do you want to avoid that kind of indebtedness, but also you don't want to burden him with the embarrassment of unnecessary *on* (the opposite of *giri*), which he would be very nervous of redeeming with an esteemed client. Who knows, you could give him an ulcer from worrying about how to release you of your obligation without appearing either grasping or patronizing.

So don't hand over your old oven-toaster: give it a decent private burial in the freshness and tranquillity of Japanese nature. As it slowly rusts away, it will release poisonous chemicals into the ground, or a hiker may stumble against it and catch tetanus from a gash caused by a sharp edge. Why, one of its reflective parts may cast the sun's rays through a dewdrop on to a dry spot that has been protected from the rain by another appliance and initiate a vast forest fire. You will have made your mark on Japanese history.

Why Loudspeakers?

The Japanese are often accused of copying or plagiarizing the inventions of other countries, but it can hardly be denied that in the field of loudspeakers they are streets ahead of any other nation. They are rightly proud of this, and lose no opportunity to show off their expertise in this branch of technology to the ears of the public — willing or unwilling. If you see something ugly, you can close your eyes or look away, but there's little you can do to a sudden blast of sound: you're literally a captive audience.

Just think of all the different places loudspeakers are to
be found, and the different uses to which they are put.
They are attached to utility poles, just out of reach of indig-
nant wire-clippers, to lure customers into everything from
pawnshops to porn shops. Police cars boom out the
registration numbers of illegally parked cars to the surrounding population of innocent bystanders, sleeping infants,
sick old folk — everybody except the miscreant driver, who
is playing *pachinko* and can't hear the police announcement above the *pachinko* parlor's even louder broadcast of
military music. Speakers in trains tell us what side to get
off, when we can catch a connecting train, to give up our
seats to deserving cases, to follow the person in front when
getting off, not to drop chewing gum on the floor, not to
forget anything. . . .

The little earphones passengers plug into their ears are
really loudspeakers in disguise, intended to broadcast the
beating of drums and cymbals to anyone within ten feet.
Wash-pole traders, wastepaper trucks and sweet potato
sellers patrol the streets with their highly amplified traditional calls, and the occasional mobile shop will blast the
unsuspecting paper doors with a compulsory dose of
Beethoven, or *enka,* or its own nerve-racking jingle — all
this under the deranged impression that the imposition of
excessive decibels will drum up more trade than it frightens
away.

Loudspeakers at temples tell visitors of the Buddhist vir-
tue of silence, while visitors to nature parks can hear taped
bird calls, to the probable confusion of the real birds whose

calls are drowned out by advanced technology. Airplanes bearing the loudest loudspeakers of all buzz residential areas exhorting the population to buy more furniture, or post their New Year cards early — at least that's what it sounds like, but you have to listen very carefully to make out what the infernal racket actually means.

Now, this might be good listening comprehension practice for the *gaijin* studying Japanese, but there is no indication the ordinary Japanese person in the street does listen carefully, or even hear these sounds any more. After all, were these exhortations actually heeded, wouldn't furniture stores be perpetually crowded, wouldn't there be an end to pushing in the trains, wouldn't those wash-poles be snapped up within minutes? If people actually take notice of those anouncements, why do Japanese railway companies have some of the world's biggest lost property departments?

Electric megaphones are now sold to beggars in Africa, adding a high-tech angle to their ancient trade, but in general, Japan needs no export outlet for its loudspeaker products. There is a big enough market of crooks and insensitive idiots at home.

Why Panic?

Why do the Japanese panic in earthquakes? Does familiarity really breed contempt? Not in the case of Japanese confronted with earthquakes, certainly.

The logic of the earthquake situation should be clear to

anyone. Panic is the last thing you want when the light starts swinging and the *kokeshi* come bouncing off the shelf on to your head. There are too many things to be done and to look out for in a short time. And surely Japanese should be used to earthquakes by now and take them calmly in their stride? After all, they queue for hours for the privilege of paying to ride a roller coaster. Not so.

Foreigner: But why do you panic?

Japanese: Because we understand how bad the damage from an earthquake can be. Buildings fall down, there are fires, etc., etc.

Foreigner: Then you should be the best prepared and the calmest when an earthquake comes. What good does it do panicking?

Japanese: I'm not panicking, I'm hiding.

Foreigner: Why under the table?

Japanese: In case the roof falls in.

Foreigner: Why don't you wear a helmet?

Japanese: No time to put it on.

Foreigner: But surely you're supposed to put out the gas?

Japanese: Yes, but I'm busy getting under the table.

Foreigner: You don't want a fire, do you?

Japanese: No, but I just can't think of everything during an earthquake.

Foreigner: Because you're panicking.

Japanese: That's not panicking. It's self-protection.

A sense of fatalism, surely a very Oriental characteristic, remains potent. Department stores can make a good profit out of ever-ready earthquake emergency packs to hang by the front door, although the majority of Japanese remain blissfully without them, despite the rush on packs immediately after a big earthquake. Anyway, not really much sense in having your pack near the door when the safest place is supposed to be the toilet. Going outside, with or without a cushion on your head, would not seem advisable anyway.

So, preparedness is much talked about but little acted upon. The moment itself is the real test. And what use to anyone, including themselves, are the people huddled together under the heaviest table, shaking hopelessly and hoping the thing will go away soon? Most people in earthquakes are killed by unreinforced concrete walls lower than two meters, or falling dolls and bookcases. Earthquake-related fires are much more easily avoided these days.

The solution? Calmly switch off the gas, retire to the toilet and make sure there is a good supply of reading matter ready there in case the roof falls in on top of the people under the table. Just beware of cisterns above your head.

And whenever there is a real emergency, avoid any nearby Japanese.

Why Cockroaches?

The scene is all too familiar: a hapless new arrival in Japan from more temperate and less humid climes stands petrified in the middle of a *tatami* room confronted by that scourge of these latitudes, the giant black cockroach (*Blatta orientalis*, or one of its close American cousins). To blat the beast out of existence or not, that is the question. But human immobility prevails. The humble, relatively harmless insect with its active antennae goes about its exploratory business: down the wall, past the bookcase and then behind the new stereo, hopefully never to be seen again.

But the fact that *gokiburi* reappear every summer in nearly every house in Japan doesn't say much for Japanese technology. It does, however, say a lot about Japanese business.

You can smash mosquitoes all summer and they'll still be back next year. It's the same with the cockroaches, against whom a whole battery of sprays, poison bombs, cockroach cottages and old slippers have been directed. Why aren't they effective? Because cockroaches are a valuable resource of great profit.

It was the brewers who started it all. They soon realized that cockroaches are partial to beer — whether the taste, the smell or the aftereffects is not clear. A brewery seemed to be a roach paradise, and it didn't need much imagination to add a flavor of hops to any device designed to lure and trap the insect. Inebriation leading to incarceration.

A clever idea this was, nonetheless. Some cockroaches, and not a few other less undesirable insects, are attracted to traps and die during the beer-tasting. Others don't actually die, they just stick there waiting to be carried off to the local garbage dump, where no doubt a few escape and further the species in a new, insalubrious location. But the important thing for the manufacturers is that they are anyway trapped in the first place: ''Let's see how many we've got today. Oh, look at them all struggling! They're really effective, these things. I didn't know we had so many cockroaches!''

Precisely. That's the point. The devices serve to attract cockroaches more than they destroy them. The better-educated roaches, graduates of embassy kitchens and Chinese restaurants, enjoy the smell of the forbidden fruit, but are not tempted to partake thereof. The result — bigger, better, cleverer, stronger cockroaches lurking just round the corner inside the house (yours, not theirs).

This is the appalling reality of this little corner of the mighty business world: kill a few to encourage their betters. It's an easy way to make money if you can get away with it. But just remember one thing: you rarely see as many cockroaches wandering around in your apartment as you find stuck in your cockroach cottage, and because of that you assume the *gokiburi* family is rapidly diminishing in number. Your logic is suspect.

The moral is: leave them alone and they'll probably go next door.

Why Sink So Low?

A perfect way to get backache is to wash up a huge load of dishes in a Japanese sink. Even Japanese have been known to complain about the height of sinks and wash-basins. The only ones who definitely don't are those Meiji and Taisho matrons who are only 120 cm tall anyway and for whom presumably the kitchen interiors were designed in the first place.

The wheels of change grind exceeding slow in the governmental standards departments, and the result is that many features of daily life no longer fit the very consumers who have to buy and use them. It is exasperating to the Japanese and foreigners alike.

Let's face it/them, the Japanese are getting bigger, whether it be in terms of height, length of inside trouser leg or general vital statistics. Experts have suggested that, for all we know, the Japanese might one day turn out to be a nation of giants. It's heading that way already. King Size departments flourish, buses are having to be redesigned with more leg room, and one day the standards for *tatami* and door lintels will have to go too. But the sinks remain.

Now if you take an average height Japanese female (the average Japanese male is rarely seen near a sink) and put her beside your average sink you will find that her 160 cm (and getting bigger) will be twice the height of the top of the sink. The actual washing zone can be at least 15 cm lower than that. The result is backache. Now your average American of 175 cm or more has to lean over something like 105 cm to reach the dishes. This could also explain the related question of why the Japanese suffer so much from stiff shoulders.

The ideal sink or washbasin will start from navel height or higher, as most people's arms operate better above that level. Moreover, in the case of face-washing, the higher the sink the less the splash. But there we come up against another traditional restraint, or lack of one. It has always been possible to splash joyfully in the Japanese washing area with no carpets or thin ceilings to worry about. Designers of bowls, sinks and baths have therefore concerned themselves not a jot with the splash factor. Nor do they now. The most expensive washbasin with gold-plated taps in your most expensive club in the Ginza rapidly becomes an amphibious zone.

This could also explain the curious way Japanese people do the washing-up. Soap all items first, then rinse off, and often in cold water. They obviously find that the simple process of soaping and rinsing item by item in hot water leaves water and suds all over the floor. This leads to another problem: if you don't use hot water or a tea-towel, how do you guarantee that all the washing detergent is removed from the crockery? Not to worry. We all know that Japanese detergent is highly poisonous — try squibbing some on a cockroach.

Why Stiff Shoulders?

The Arabs have lots of words for camels, the Mongols have lots of words for horses and the Japanese have a special word for stiff shoulders. Clearly it is an important word, too, because it crops up all over the place all the time. But is the fact that the word *katakori* exists somehow connected to the fact that everyone seems to suffer? We all know that once a problem has been defined in Japan, everyone gets involved.

Now what could cause stiff shoulders? It might be too much slaving over a low sink or too much typing, or pillows that are either too hard, too soft or too few in number (all three of which are common). Whatever it is, the fact of announcing that one has indeed got stiff shoulders leads to the inevitable response of ''Oh, let me give you a massage!''

The inevitable conclusion is that the Japanese want to touch more and be touched, and massage is a perfectly neutral form of touching hardly likely to raise an eyebrow. Age, sex or political tendencies seem to have no bearing on the matter. However, there is the oft-repeated idea that kimonos are cut that way because men find the nape of a woman's neck desirable, and a good massage is the best way of having intimate contact with the nape, so to speak. So that might also play a part.

Another reason could be the very act of massage itself. Japan is full of grandmother-trained amateur masseuses who claim to know sufficient not to damage, only to soothe. But any self-appointed devotee of the gentle art of *shiatsu* should be treated with caution. Even professionals have been known to break their thumbs applying the pressure — so what happens to the patient? It could be a self-perpetuating form of punishment.

But there is one more possibility in the way of an explanation. It could be the fault of that most wonderful Japanese invention, the bath. The *o-furo* is undoubtedly good for every part of the body except the neck. Even though, in theory, the hottest water is always at the top, the neck tends to be the least effectively submerged part, and it's certainly the last in and first out. There is also the shape of the bath to take into consideration. When properly immersed, the body tends to lean either on the neck or the shoulders, whereas in a Western bath the more normal bathing position gives support to the back as well. And, unless the bath is made of stainless steel, the bath surface at that point is likely to be much cooler than the actual water.

QED ? Who can tell? Perhaps the real answer is a combination of these, plus the fact that the Japanese are, without question, a nation of hypochondriacs. We've already seen how athlete's foot becomes something to really worry about when pictures of it greet you outside the chemist's. And so it may be with stiff shoulders. We can't speak for Bushmen (who probably get stiff shoulders from peering up into the sky waiting for Japanese airmen to drop Coca-Cola bottles) or Eskimos (who get their physical kicks from rubbing noses), but most humans do seem to get stiff necks quite often. They just don't make a big fuss about it.

Perhaps we should just blame it all on the kimono. No wonder those unmarried girls at Meiji Shrine all wear fur stoles at the New Year. They prefer not to be touched.

Why Croaking Pigeons?

You would expect pigeons to coo rather than croak, but in Japan they croak. A devout Buddhist might suggest it's the result of recycling the lives of so many frogs lost to the drying up of so many rice paddies turned into parking lots and housing developments. That answer must remain conjecture, however, due to the difficulty of confirmation — although the logic is impeccable. While nobody expects pigeons to have the clear tones of mourning doves, no one can be prepared for the death rattle of Japanese pigeons. Even though some in Mexico City can gasp almost as convincingly, they can be written off as suffering from the rarefied air combined with using Spanish R's and the fear of earthquakes, the only common denominator.

All the pigeons we can hear in Japan, however, seem to be gargling something. It could be attributed to using a different language (as with Japanese crows who say "*kā-kā*" rather than "caw-caw"). Yet, even ducks and geese in Japan respond to the same calls that are used in North America.

Nevertheless an Anglo-Franco, Italo-Greco "coo-coo" is more likely to be answered by a genuine cuckoo than a pigeon in Japan. Indeed, you can be perceived as genuinely cuckoo if you persist in attempting to use "coo-coo" for a pigeon. It's easy to see how these phenomena fit a cartoon scenario for cross-cultural miscommunication:

Homer Pigeon flies in on a cross-current jet stream (via Anchorage) and asks directions while perched on the famed monument of the ever faithful dog, Hachiko, outside Tokyo's Shibuya Station:

"Clear your throat, man! I can't make out a [expletive deleted] thing!"

Then it becomes crystal-clear as he tries again at the south end of the station atop the sign that faithfully reports CO, NO_3 and other noxious conditions in parts per million or degrees centigrade.

"*Naruhodo*, they're suffering from air pollution!"

Nevertheless, there is evidence that they may have

sounded like this before chronic air pollution. Older Japanese insist on the correctness of "*pohp-pohp-poh*" to represent the call of Japanese *hato*. They sound the same in Kyoto, as well, far from salt air and factory exhaust . . . could it be from frustration as all the temples string up wires and netting to cover all convenient perches? Toy ceramic whistles in the shape of pigeons, *hatobue*, widely distributed since Edo times, are capable of both "coo-coo" and *pohp-poh,* depending on how you blow or tongue them.

The true answer may be as biologists explain genetic drift as a result of long-term isolation. Certainly ever since the extinction (mass extermination) of the migratory passenger pigeon and the institution of modern quarantines, international communication among pigeons has been greatly curtailed. (Advanced Star-War technology, on the other hand, may restore the utility of homing pigeons used for clandestine activities from long before Edo times.)

In any event, when you've lived in Japan long enough you get to think *pohp-pohp-poh* is perfectly natural and that "coo-coo" must be an aberration!

IX
Officials and Officialdom

Why Ugly Faces?

Why do election posters always bear such ugly faces? Like Oliver Cromwell, who insisted on having his portrait painted "with warts and all," Japanese politicians are ruthlessly honest even to the point of self-degradation. This runs even to the extent of having election posters with ugly faces for all to see. For this they should be respected and admired throughout the civilized world.

Every candidate in an election is fully aware that he would win hands down if he had posters printed with a panda, a koala, a frilled lizard, an axolotl or some similar cute beast momentarily in fashion, but no, that core of viciously determined integrity will not allow him to stoop so low. Instead, they all have their own portraits pinned up in colors lurid enough to turn the stomach of the most hardened voter. Some even pose in baseball caps, or holding incongruous objects like wrenches that they've never used in their lives, just to make themselves look even more ridiculous.

In this way, the official notice boards at election time look like a veritable Rogues' Gallery of thugs and delinquents, showing off to the unsuspecting electorate their shifty eyes, debauched features and, if they have the audacity to smile, their misshapen, rotten teeth repaired in gold that must have cost a fortune in the bribes that everybody knows Japanese politicians never accept. Sometimes you see pictures of candidates posing with a *daruma*. Remember that the *daruma* is the one not holding

the paintbrush.

And what is the message from all this? It is, of course, Personal Integrity. By revealing himself or herself to the voters in this way, every candidate is saying, in effect: ''I know that nobody in his right mind would buy a used car from somebody looking like me, but I am sufficiently honest and straightforward to admit it. I hope that you will respect and admire this honesty and straightforwardness of mine. They are both qualities that are essential to the future of Japanese politics, and I humbly beg you to vote for me. I will not bore you with my policies, or indeed with the policies of my party; please just remember the courage required to put this mug of mine in front of a camera, and vote. My name, by the way, is that string of characters next to my left ear. I have put my name in *hiragana* rather than *kanji* to show how little respect I have for your level of literacy. Thank you. Vote for me, and then get lost.''

Why No Army?

This is for the same reason there is no air force or navy: it's against the law. What a wonderful idea! If every country in the world followed the example set by Japan, and inserted in its constitution a clause outlawing military forces, what a different world it would be! But alas, even Japan does not have the courage of its constitutional convictions, and in fact operates something that any casual observer can easily see bears more than a passing resemblance to fully fledged military forces. To get round that pesky clause, they are called by the two-faced name of Self-Defense Forces. Who ever heard of any country honest enough to call its army Offense Forces anyway?

The Self Defense referred to is not the traditional martial arts like *karate*, *judo* or *aikido*, but the latest in modern weaponry, short of nuclear arms. These are also against the law in Japan: they cannot be used, produced or "introduced" into the country. The government are very, very strict on this, even insisting that the U.S. should have prior consultations with them before nuclear-armed vessels dock at U.S. bases in Japan. Since there have never been any consultations, it stands to reason that no U.S. ships carrying nuclear weapons have ever entered a Japanese port. And if you'll believe that, may we interest you in the world rights for marketing a revolutionary new left-handed screwdriver?

The U.S. provides a lot of Japanese military equipment, but now more and more is being produced at home, by companies not dissimilar to the arms combines that made such a killing in World War II. Indeed, some Japanese weapons technology is so advanced the U.S. wants to buy it, but can't — selling arms technology is against the law, too. And the big arms combines, being peace-loving subjects of a peace-loving nation with a peace-loving constitution, are only too happy to obey this law.

In terms of the total annual sum spent on "defense," Japan ranks in the world's top ten. For per capita spending, it is further down the ratings. And the country is way, way down near the bottom as far as proportion of GNP allotted to military expenditure is concerned, whether or not it goes above Prime Minister Miki's 1976 self-imposed ceiling of one percent. You choose the statistics according to the point you want to make.

Actually, annual expenditure on expense account entertainment is higher than that for defense. How would you like your money squandered, dear consumer — laser-guided missiles blasting hell out of what remains of the Japanese countryside on the SDF practice ranges halfway up ex-sacred Mount Fuji, or mounds of expensive sushi served with vintage Scotch by smiling maidens to fat cats who leave most of their expensive fare to be thrown out and turned into landfill?

Why Fingerprinting?

Or to put it as many newcomers see it, why are resident Koreans, foreign journalists, Protestant missionaires,

Catholic clergy, and foreigners married to Japanese getting bent over such a minor thing as recording the pattern of their left index finger? Why have thousands already refused to do it? Well, everyone involved and most critics realize the fingerprint isn't really what counts.

For each side it is a principle, but the principles involved are at odds. Foreigners who object to the refusers wonder at the lack of rationality, since they share none of the assumptions held but have threatened interests of their own. In short, all positions are held in self-interest but with differing perceptions of "self" and what is "good."

It is worth pointing out that social problems and circumstances are quite similar throughout the developed world and that differences are matters of degree and proportion. Historically, Japan remains close to strict authoritarianism; law is entirely discretionary and a closed process, little open to public scrutiny or oversight.

Any failure to obey authority is a sign of a deterioration of the social order; it is obvious these refusers are a real threat to society and Japan's stability. It's bad enough that foreigners on their own soil try to tell the Japanese what they should do for government, education and economic policy — but on Japanese soil?

The refusers see themselves as either victims of a vindictive reversal of citizenship law after sovereignty was returned to Japan by the Allied powers, or as supporters of those victims coming from traditions of social protest ranging from forcing Magna Carta out of King John to Martin Luther's 95 Theses, the French Revolution, Nazi resistance or Thoreau's different drummer. To refusers, this obviously unjust law must be protested and the government taught a lesson in the tradition of Gandhi or Nobel Laureate Martin Luther King Jr.

Of course, objectors to the refusers object because they don't want to be tarred with a brush that could threaten their own hard-won opportunities in Japan.

The government sees itself making grand concessions in a more "flexible" alien registration policy for 1988, while the refusers assert that the more things change the more they stay the same. That is, maximum penalties are not removed and ID cards (instead of pass-books) must still be carried by all aliens over sixteen. All can see the inequity of Japan's case-by-case administration of law when it penalizes an American woman married to a Japanese only a few bucks while it detains a Korean man married to a Japanese citizen during deportation proceedings.

Japan's world citizenship will eventually even out discrepancies in rights and privileges even as socialist and capitalist countries adjust their respective social and economic policies. At least something can be said for abandoning ancient traditions of boiling in oil or use of dungeons as featured in the film *Shogun,* in favor of a teeny-weeny little card. Given Japanese reliance on tradition, something could even be said for expunging those ancient practices from Japanese history books!

Why Police Boxes?

There can be no doubt that the Japanese neighborhood policing system is the envy of the world. Whether policing is so effective because there is hardly any crime anyway, or there is hardly any crime because policing is so effective, is difficult to establish, but suffice it to say that Singapore has expressed an interest in introducing the system of police *kōban*. Yes, Singapore, where police surveillance has already been honed down to the fine art of stopping and fining on the spot anyone who drops so much as a cigarette butt in the street. And indeed Japan does have a venerable tradition of strict control over the activities of each and every member of any neighborhood — a tradition that survives not only in the existence of your friendly local police box, but also in tightly knit residents' associations that impose a subtle but inexorable social authority.

For the cop himself, sitting in the *kōban* with his boots off, warming his feet against the kerosene stove that is at the same time boiling the water for interminable cups of *o-cha*, this is the life! Better this than pounding the beat like the poor old coppers have to do in countries where there is no such thing as a *kōban*. Better than sitting astride a noisy motorbike being splashed with mud by trucks and having your ears assaulted by radio instructions from HQ every five seconds. And we don't know what the actual regulations are, but our own observations would indicate that the occasional drag on a cigarette is permitted.

But what do these *kōban* hermits do? When they're

there, that is, for more and more seem to be empty after dark, in other words at those times when crimes might be considered more likely to occur. What do they do? Well, er, they, er, well, for one thing they give directions. The police box by the statue of Hachiko at Shibuya Station has the record for numbers of instructions given. But couldn't ordinary citizens perform that service? Oh, no, just try it some time. In fact, policemen are just as ignorant caught away from the *kōban*: what helps them in their little box is a map, hung on the wall amongst the Wanted posters, lost gloves and riot equipment. All right, they give directions. So what else? Oh, well, they, er, occasionally put on their hard helmets, pick up little clipboards and cycle leisurely round to make sure the local bank hasn't been robbed. Then they pedal back, take off those uncomfortable helmets, sit down, scratch their feet and have another cup of tea. Which all goes to show they're human, and a good thing, too.

Because if they weren't hanging around being lazy, they might be marching around in riot gear, raring for a fight with any group of fellow citizens they might happen to decide were being unruly. They might be banging on the doors of innocent people at dead of night to take their fingerprints, or intimidating the populace with militaristic parades, march-pasts and similar shows of strength. And we wouldn't want that to happen, would we? No, the *kōban*s are a good thing. They keep the fuzz off the streets.

Why Flashing?

Even when not in hot pursuit of hoodlums, you rarely see a *patokā* in motion without an array of flashing red lights front and back and on the roof. In the same way, an ambulance with its sirens off, even on a deserted road, is unusual enough to turn your head — although the unnecessarily blaring sirens do turn your head much more. You begin to wonder if Japanese police cars and ambulances aren't made by the same companies that produced those tin-and-plastic Made-in-Japan toy cars of your childhood: push them and they make a noise.

Cynics would suggest, as they do in every country, that

the driver turns on the flashing lights so he can get a clear run through the traffic and get back before his dinner gets cold. But is that really so? He's probably going to have *bento* to eat, and that's got to be cold anyway; and if he wants a cup of tea he knows there's always, but always, one brewing at his nearest *kōban*. So what's the hurry? Indeed, you often see them, lights aflash so as to put even the neon signs of Shinjuku in the shade, not speeding along the highway but just crawling, snail's pace, obeying the speed limit that looks slow even as miles per hour and is even slower in k.p.h. Now, why do that?

The answer is in the adage: prevention is better than cure. No motorist in his right mind is going to overtake one of these flashing, flickering slowcoaches; result — a tailback of law-abiding motorists, all driving just on the speed limit, and gnashing their teeth in frustrated agony. The flashing lights work, and in a country that has actually cut its traffic death rates while seeing its numbers of vehicles increase in geometric leaps and bounds, this is no mean consideration. Certainly, they work better than those plastic model cops that are erected to guard major danger spots — usually minus a limb or two and standing in a mound of filth and detritus that makes you wonder whether the Japanese people really do have a deep sense of respect for their police force.

And that's the reason why Japanese speed traps are the kindest in the world. You can spot them miles away, as a fully flashing *patokā* lurks ostentatiously round a corner. The only trouble comes if it decides to lurk next to a gas stand, in which case it camouflages itself neatly with the similar strobes and garish illumination of the gas stand. If in doubt, pretend you're stopping to fill up.

But in the end, doesn't it all boil down to a refutation of that myth about the Japanese and their group identity, modesty, hammer-down-the-nail-that-sticks-up mentality and all that? The fact is, the same happens to Japanese people as happens to any other nationality when you put them in uniform and give them a little authority. They like to show off. We all like to show off. When you're momentarily disoriented by all those lights or deafened by those seemingly superfluous sirens, the first reaction is to want to kick in the lights, sirens and heads of the perpetrators, but sit yourself behind the wheel of one of those vehicles, and can you promise to resist the temptation to flick those switches? Surely no one will mind, just for a few seconds, will they?

Why Longevity?

Given one of the world's longest life expectancies, it is natural to expect that medical science plays an important role in Japanese longevity. In fact, however, it would seem to be in spite of rather than because of Japanese medicine, something like nature healing faster than medication. After all, antibiotics have yet to cure a viral infection anywhere in the world. But the Japanese national health service ensures more people get medical attention than, say, in the U.S. with its more plentiful and better trained physicians — but also more antibiotics for viruses.

Crediting Japan's Ministry of Health and Welfare for Japanese longevity is akin to crediting the atomic bomb for the same phenomenon. Like most bureaucracies the world over, the MHW in Japan is capable of some gross stupidities. Not the least among them is its peculiar respect for ''authority'' (Japanese, only) over scientific evidence. The long delay in approving polio vaccine has given Japan one of the youngest groups of victims among developed nations. Early approval of thalidomide but delayed acceptance of vaccine against measles invites discomforting comparison of which resulting defects are worse. Interrupted use of whooping-cough vaccine prevented a handful of deaths that may have resulted from careless administration but assured that thousands would die of whooping cough and infection levels remain among the highest in industrialized countries. Abortion still prevails over the pill (evoking shades of infanticide charges). These are all well publicized. Less publicized absurdities (like scientifically useless toxicity tests that make raising beagles very profitable) would fill this book many times over.

Poor education of the public as well as doctors ensures Japan will keep a lower place in the world rankings than is deserved by the truly competent. Six years' study and one year (down from two) of supervised practice can never compare with ten and four as is the norm in the States. Unquestioningly following doctors' orders only worsens the effects of ignorance. Health insurance administration penalizes a doctor for giving only good advice, but rewards prescribing high-cost medication. Of course, responsible doctors do give good advice, but who can blame them for recommending a relatively safe medication "just in case?" Other MHW policies encourage use of less effective "new" medication over more reliable standbys (such as zinc powder for athlete's foot!).

The worst-case example involves the retro-viruses HTLV I, II and III. HTLV-III is AIDS, while I and II are causes of various cancers long regarded unique to Japan. Testing for HTLV-III was approved within weeks of the media panic about AIDS, while pressure to test for the other two has been steadily resisted. Finally with approval to test for all three, only the few hundred AIDS carriers will be informed and counseled. Millions of HTLV-I or -II carriers will not even be informed, although the advice should be the same (have regular checkups and prevent the exchange of bodily fluids that carry the virus — blood, milk or semen). Some expert even said in print (in Japanese) that HTLV-I-infected blood was OK to donate to elderly patients since it took a few years for leukemia to develop! Need we say more?

Why So Many *Sensei?*

Without a respect system, the average traditionally-minded Japanese would be at a total loss. Classification of people depends on age, university year (not graduation, that can take too long), position, rank, experience, etc., etc. This accounts for the desperate questioning of foreigners who from mere appearance alone are unclassifiable.

But the greatest classification of all is *sensei.* We can roughly translate this eminently flexible and useful word as follows: "actual teacher, master or instructor; supposed teacher, master or instructor; actual expert; supposed expert; self-professed expert; Traditional Japanese Arts con-artist; person with experience; any type of doctor; person worthy of respect; person who demands respect and money; person somehow better than me; proficient person; person in beret; person habitually late for lesson; person habitually absent from lesson; person who has appeared on NHK; person who has lived in Paraguay, Tibet or Bulgaria; person who paints in Paris; person whose name I can't remember. . . ."

The flexibility of the word explains its ubiquitous quality. English is so lacking in this kind of expression which can shape one's whole relationship with people. It is in the same class as *senpai* and *kōhai.* Given the fact that although 99.5 percent of Japanese are middle-class there is in fact no equality except between classmates, then a simple calculation will show that the great majority of Japanese must have or be a *sensei*. The reason that English has no equivalent is that we lack respect. The aim of any self-respecting Westerner is to get on first-name terms with anyone and everyone to prove that in fact we can all pretend to be equal under law and heaven. That is the last thing a Japanese really wants.

Mere association with a *sensei,* particularly a *dai-sensei* (the most important subcategory), brings its rewards. Take the example of the well-known TV Conversation *sensei* who is theoretically, or perhaps incidentally, a genuine University *Dai-Sensei*. To be listed as in his class is a privilege, even an honor, and certainly meaningful to others.

Student: Oh, he's a wonderful *sensei*.

Gaijin: But he is a busy public figure. Does he ever turn up for classes?

Student: Not often, but we do.

Gaijin: But does he teach you anything?

Student: He is our *sensei*.

Gaijin: Ah.

This leads us to perhaps the most important point about *sensei*: once a *sensei,* always a *sensei,* and therefore always worthy of respect. Look at the God of Niigata, ex-Prime Minister Kakuei Tanaka. Any real supporter, colleague or voter (of which there are millions) will always refer to him as "Tanaka *Sensei*" or just "*Sensei*." Why? Because he is the man who pulls the strings, who makes the impossible dream a reality, who makes life better and more rewarding by whatever means for those who are not *sensei*. A man who can be re-elected from his sickbed and halfway to jail proves he is a real *sensei*.

Sensei is God.

Why Education Reform?

Although nobody understands the system, including the Japanese, Japanese education has been the object of world-wide attention. For the Japanese the issues seem to be, in the main, examination hell, *ijime* or bullying, *juku* or cram schools, suicide, morality and education reform. In the West, vis-à-vis Japanese "strengths," the concerns are math scores, overall literacy, private school alternatives, total school days, average hours of homework and, yes, education reform. Asian neighbors' concern over textbook "reforms" is another matter.

Since everyone wants to keep the good and throw away the bad, you might expect a combination of both perspectives might yield an ideal system. But it does not work out that way. Both share much of what they want to throw away while also prizing what the other despises. There seems to be little awareness that with the particular merit of a system the good comes with the bad as part of an integrated whole. Take away either the examination hell or cram schools and watch math scores tumble. Take away free time and flexibility and watch creativity wither on the vine.

Japanese education does not only rely on rote memory,

but is strictly authoritarian, discouraging questions in the classroom, much less encouraging discussion and challenging inquiry — how can they with over forty students per class? Students come to school exhausted, learn but little, go to cram school, do double homework until late and rise early. The routine is repeated daily for a sentence of six years culminating in examinations for parole at college, which all too often turns out to be a self-execution. College students who made parole at last play, play, play; some company will complete their education after graduation and teach them to be workaholic, alcoholic or both.

Knowledge is fragmented: Japanese history is in *nengō* but Western history in Gregorian calendar dates and never the twain shall meet. All students learn the relation of the earth's movements and the seasons, day length, etc., but adults still labor under the impression that Japan's four seasons are unique, while the truly unique feature of a small country spanning alpine to tropical climates goes unnoticed.

Thus, while some may argue that efficient storage of data in early years prepares for future creativity, it appears that simply avoiding garbage *in* does not ensure against natural fertilizers *out*. Ignorant authority prevails over informed science. Books are judged by their covers. "Scholars" exult in reasoning with feeling instead of logic. Internationalization is coordinated with guidelines to ignore international pronunciation. By no means are inconsistencies unique to Japan, but these are easy to spot and criticize.

Mr. Nakasone's world-class blunder in 1986 revealed

him, too, to be a typical product of the education system he wants to reform. His ignorant comments about multi-ethnic cultures received international press attention, but his accompanying conclusion that Japan had excelled for thousands of years on its own was even more revealing. How had Japan excelled? Longest Stone Age? Last rice grower? Best raw fish? And in relation to whom? Who'll reform the educators while the educators are busy reforming education?

X
Cults and Culture

Why Geisha?

The inevitable question is, are they prostitutes? The answer never satisfies, but must remain, no, but. . .

The origin of *geisha* (artisans, literally) can probably be traced to Chinese Tang or Song/Sung dynasty court dancers and entertainers. Of course, on Japanese soil, the institution developed its own character and identity. Hostesses evolved in modern times as Everyman's "geisha," no experience required — actually no way related except in the superficial point of being paid to serve customers.

So the crux of the inevitable question is who pays for what, how. Employers of geisha or hostesses pay salary with bonuses or an hourly wage for professional or layman services. Customers pay the respective proprietor for food, drinks and cover charges at rates that pay for the cost of delivering service plus a, presumably, modest to handsome profit. (At $200 a head and up for an evening that ends before midnight, we wonder if it isn't time to chuck our word-crunchers and rent a square meter or two in downtown Tokyo!) If customers get more, they pay for it where they get it, when they get it.

A look at the scene in Western society provides an adequate analogy. Las Vegas night spots, for example, provide both entertainers and companionable servers. No one ever confuses big-name singers or dancers with prostitutes. And are we to assume bar girls and go-go dancers of recent fashion were prostitutes for accepting whiskey prices for iced tea? Are Marilyn Monroe, Liz Taylor or Zsa Zsa Gabor, who all certainly got around, professional entertainers, or what? Are all, some or any professional entertainers or cocktail service personnel required or expected to be prostitutes? Answers to these questions, however qualified, reflect corresponding insight into the Japanese scene.

The only enigmatic point about geisha results from anachronistic feudal customs regarding their training, apprenticeship and working contracts. It's almost as if professional entertainers were required to work tables a few years before being permitted to work exclusively on stage. On both a scale of popularity or artistic achievement a geisha's accomplishments should rank somewhere between classic jazz and operatic arias combined with the wit and grace of Julia Childs and Miss Manners. Not exactly entertainment for the masses but as respectable as ever can be itemized on any expense account.

While hostesses have only a superficial similarity to geisha in serving drinks, they are beginning to fill the entertainment gap as "go-go singers" with customers and the ubiquitous *karaoke*. Still, no experience needed, much less an apprenticeship, so college students often fill the bill.

The steamier side of sexploitation is in steamy baths and with imports . . . it's easier to exploit the insecurity of a homeless entertainer-to-be . . . but, then, they are neither geisha nor legal hostesses; also, many people are taking home a lot more than they paid for. Vindictive moralizers say they are finally paying.

Why Soapland?

Contrary to the way it sounds, "Soapland" is not a clean business, although it is cleaning up on more than its customers' wallets. One of the first steps in cleaning up their act was to adopt the euphemism "Soapland" as a corrective to the offensive use of *toruko* (for "Turkish," but also synonymous with Turkey).

Since Japanese "Turkish baths" had become world-famous for things infamous and offensive to any adherent to the Islamic faith (if not the Christian faith), the term was guaranteed to raise the ire of traditionally Islamic Turks. Turkish Christians didn't find the appellation amusing, either, for that matter. Even secularly minded Turkish businessmen who could sense an element of goodwill engendered in their Japanese counterparts by such associations still felt the minuses of leering grins, sotto voce inquiries, etc., far outweighed any gains.

Finally, after years of complaints from the backs of taxis to diplomatic receptions, one of Turkey's ambassadors caught the ear of the press and the eye of the public. This focus of attention made the tightly held and, at least nominally regulated, "flesh trade" reconsider the need to replace all of their old and new flashing neon, tons of handbills and square kilometers of advertising layouts, etc., to, in short, create a new image.

Now timing seems to be of the essence here, since the change followed the successful introduction of Disneyland. So, if the exotic flavor of the Bosporus where East literally meets West was forever to be lost, what could appeal more than the allusion to Mickey's Fantasy Land or Peter Pan's Never-Never Land? And what could be more clean fun while refurbishing a tarnished image? So, Soapland it is and probably so for at least as long as it was "Turkish."

As Japanese institutions go, Soapland's precursor was youthful, indeed, with perhaps three decades at most before the name change. Dictionaries and encyclopedias don't presume to be authoritative about the things that every second-grader can learn on the playground, so it is not clear when "baths in the Islamic tradition" (in one family dictionary) became a "sex service" pleasure spot (in an annual guide to contemporary language). Having graduated from American and English playgrounds, we can't presume to know more than the encyclopedias, either, except for consulting Japanese comics which are the texts from Japanese playgrounds. After meandering through Greco-Roman public baths and Finnish saunas, one popular multivolume set fixes 1953 as the year of the first genuine Turkish bath, 1958 as a year of nationwide proliferation of pseudo-operations, with "saunas" — which persist to the present — beginning about 1966.

Like Disneyland, the modified concept appears to come from the U.S. of A. Timing seems to have decided who would operate these establishments. Coming so soon after the war, only illicit capital must have been available for such rapid expansion. Whatever the case, Japan's organized crime has been closely associated with this popular hit with the public. Yet, we wonder if it would still be called Soapland under different management.

Why *Karaoke?*

Everyone is excited, one way or another, about *karaoke*, because it is difficult to stay neutral, especially when TV networks sponsor regular contests. At least one channel devotes late hours to playing the latest video versions. You have the option to select a sound-channel combination to sing along solo, in duet with the featured performer or simply listen as a non-participant.

But you can't control the decibel level of most *karaoke* with remote-control switches. Hence, much of the excitement is negative and denunciatory: *karaoke* bars provide the police with the most complaints for noise pollution. It reached a peak, ominously, in 1984 when Tokyo's pink zones had to observe an 11:30 curfew. (Although that hour applied throughout the land, not all police have been as diligent in enforcement as they initially were in Shinjuku's Kabuki-cho area.)

The term means empty orchestra and the concept was inspired by the Music Minus One recordings for teaching classical musicians and operatic singers. The fad blossomed and bellowed with Japan's economic boom. Now, wherever Japanese gather, from Singapore to São Paulo, New York to Honolulu, *karaoke* is there.

Attempts were made even to market the equipment outside Japan but they have not proven successful. Those attempting to market it think the problem is an insufficient supply of appropriately canned sing-along music. We suspect that an expensive tape deck plus amp, mikes and speakers that duplicate the capability of any home stereo system wouldn't find many takers anyhow. Not to mention that people in most countries prefer making their own live music or otherwise listening and dancing to music by accomplished performers.

Perhaps this is the crux! Places where most Japanese can gather are too small for everyone to dance, much less feature live music. (Discos, where everyone can dance, don't feature *karaoke*.) Maximum participation is possible simply by passing around a mike and songbook with accompanying tapes . . . if there is space, a few might dance, but things are pretty cozy anyway.

For a brief flash, it was popular to match electronically rated performances on a scale of one to ten (actually a digital readout in percentage points). With the advent of video discs, naturally, there is a new dimension to the empty orchestra, including soft porn. There are even empty pillow scenes to accompany songs of lost love. We must confess that on a scale of one to ten *karaoke* does not have enough appeal for us to confirm whether TV carries this degree of excitement or not . . . but we do have acquaintances who can stand to watch Sunday afternoon contests featuring *gaijin* and live orchestras that sound just like the ones in the can (unintentional pun).

Why Sumo?

While baseball may literally be a thousand-fold more popular than sumo (or *Ōzumō* for Grand Sumo), this is the only sport that can be said to be Japanese in origin. Of course, the Greeks, Romans and Chinese, among others, had wrestling competitions much earlier and with similar objectives. To this day, also, there's hardly a schoolground in the world without some version of king-on-the-mountain. But no one can boast a professional organization with a continuous history like the Japanese can with their version.

And, superficially at least, it is something most foreigners can immediately understand in spite of apparent exotic uniqueness. The fact that a couple of foreigners from Hawaii have become a part of Sumodom contributes interest (and raises some important problems). There is, furthermore, something intriguing in its traditional trappings.

Beneath the questionable glamour of huge behemoths struggling like beached whales, there is a world more strictly feudal than any other traditional system in Japan. A closed and strictly regulated world, stable masters control every aspect of life for those in their charge. While top-division wrestlers get hard-won benefits, all others serve some form of servitude, waiting hand and foot on their superiors; novices haven't so much as their own spending money. There is no pretense to democracy or objectivity.

One exceptionally able Canadian left after less than two years with an undefeated record simply because he couldn't put up with so much [expletive deleted]. As he had little good to say for the system, he has been banned for life from any future participation. Two others who found a way to put up with *Nihon*-sense have reaped the rewards of go-

ing along with the system, but not without stirring up xenophobic fears or resentment.

Similar sentiments come out in baseball, where the professional teams are allowed two *gaijin* on their roster and a third in reserve. By some strange twist of logic, the Japan baseball commissioner felt only by eliminating foreigners altogether could Japan attain international standards. Where would North American baseball be without unrestricted use of foreigners in Canada or from Latin America? Sumo cannot improve its already limited reputation with such reasoning.

At any rate, Sumo is indisputably Japanese and an accessible way to find the essential spirit and fundamental ethos of the old *bushidō* (Military Way) of the samurai. Still, for those who see it for the first time, the reaction cannot be unlike that of the British royals when whisked in to see a few final matches of a few seconds' duration each (culminating prolonged rituals of posturing and tossing mounds of salt around the ring). Princess Diana's words were inaudible over the tube, but her expression belied the universal question "It's fun, but is that all there is to it?" Well, yes; but, no, when you know the rest of the story.

Why Men Only?

Ah, that's an easy one, you might well be saying to yourself. If all Kabuki actors weren't men they would be actresses, not actors! Full marks for that, but there is more to it. The reason Kabuki works so well, and here we have to risk the ire of all "Equality in Kabuki" supporters, is that actresses do not appear under normal circumstances. Although it was founded by a woman, about Shakespeare's time.

The fact that Kabuki as we know it lacks actresses is the fault of their predecessors entirely — obscene females were banned from appearing. Had it not been that way, Takarazuka might have had more opposition. But who can doubt that the development of a male tradition was a wise move?

Doubters should witness a Kabukiesque play in which women are allowed to participate. Even worse are the occasions when *onnagata* are put in the ring with actresses playing the other female parts. A perfect example of this was a run of *Othello* a few years ago in Tokyo in which the Kabuki actor Tamasaburo was arguably one of the finest Desdemonas ever in a production that was arguably the worst.

What this all means is that Kabuki, having been forced to become all-male by law, has now reached an impregnable state of all-maleness. Any attempts to breach it are misguided, and almost as bad as allowing women on a Noh stage. On the other hand, it would be marvelous to reinstate female sumo wrestlers to the *dohyo* rather than have to put up with the halfhearted efforts recently popular at beer gardens. But we are getting away from the point.

A female Kabuki character gains from being a man because the imagination of the audience comes into play: a willing suspension of disbelief is imperative when confronted with the spectacular posturing of a wizened actor such as Utaemon. An old and distinguished actress would bring a different power to the role, but it would be too close to reality. Kabuki is the theater of the unreal loosely disguised as naturalism.

To take the argument a little further, one of the weaknesses of Kabuki is that child roles are played by children. This is understandably charming to the grandmothers out in the crowd, but a child actor is always too real, too personalized. On the other hand, the child puppets of Bunraku become perfectly idealized children and therefore capable of much greater dramatic intensity and genuine theatrical emotion.

And so it is with real women acting. They bring to the

part their own femininity, their own proportions, their subjective understanding of what it is to be a woman. That is ideal for television. It is also the norm nowadays for women to play Shakespeare's female roles, but that is only because the Elizabethan form of male-only theater did not survive the passage of the centuries. The result of that loss of a traditional form has been the endless striving to make Shakespeare realistic and "meaningful." For Shakespeare's audience, the unreality of the whole stage setting and way of acting made the plays themselves surely much more accessible.

And there is a final thought, a question worth thinking about: why is it that men playing women tend to be more convincing and dramatically satisfying than women playing men, unless you happen to be a Takarazuka fan?

Why Show Faces?

There are few visitors remotely interested in theater who do not visit a Bunraku performance. They have read about the emotional intensity created by the skillful combination of the narrators who read all parts and the miniature dolls brilliantly operated by no less than three men unseen.

Unseen? Very rarely. The first shock is the fact that a lot of the time the chief puppeteer, responsible for the head and one arm, has his face fully revealed to the audience. The second is that none of the Japanese in the audience seem to worry about this, even though the human face is totally out of scale with the size of the doll's head — do they even notice?

Have the puppeteers forgotten their hoods? Clearly not. But what has happened to the well-documented *kuroko* tradition whereby operators can "become invisible" and therefore heighten the dramatic effect of the whole piece? Bunraku dolls look marvelous even in still photos when you cannot see their operators.

Let us listen in on a conversation between one such visitor (V) and a Japanese aficionado (A):

V: But who *wants* to see the same old operators' faces time and time again with different dolls? It's not as though they are ventriloquists and want to demonstrate how good they are at not moving their lips. Their job is much easier than that because someone is doing all the speaking for them.

A: Ah, but we Bunraku fans *do* want to see the operators' faces. You see, the expression on the puppeteer's face so subtly, delicately and beautifully mirrors the emotions and "expression" on the doll's face.

V: Ah, so puppeteers are frustrated actors?

A: No, no, performing *with* the doll is part of the skill.

V: In that case, why don't puppeteers around the world display themselves, too?

A: I don't know. Maybe they are shy. Maybe they do not have the skill to restrain their own emotions and facial expressions while operating.

V: Hmm. It sounds to me more as if Bunraku puppeteers have too little to do. After all, they're only working a third of the doll, so they probably get bored.

A: No, you don't understand at all. It can take 20 or 30 years to be able to operate a doll properly, working for many hours every day.

V: Thirty years? Surely anyone could do that.

A: No, no. You have to be a dedicated artist and very sensitive.

V: That's it. They're very sensitive about the fact that it takes them so long to perfect their art and they want to show the audience they're not embarrassed — wearing a hood would be loss of face!

A: You don't seem to understand at all. Some of these men are Living National Treasures, true artists.

V: But not very self-effacing ones.

A: What do you mean?

V: Well, it seems to me that they like everyone in the audience to get a good look at their face to know just who is doing what. It's rather like minor Kabuki actors in minor roles insisting on having all the lights on stage equally lit. Presumably, even after 30 years each puppeteer still doesn't have enough originality of style to make it easy to recognize him through his puppet?

A: Oh, no. We aficionados can tell who the operator is even without reading the program beforehand or seeing his face.

V: So why don't they wear their hoods, then?

Why Six Toes?

That's just what puzzled the president of the Japanese Ukiyoe Society and a colleague in the spring of 1984. They found some thirteen figures in seven plates in a famous series of woodblock prints by Ando Hiroshige, otherwise known as Utagawa Hiroshige, the most illustrious and gifted representative of the Utagawa school of *ukiyoe* — "floating-world" pictures.

Widely known by his personal name, Hiroshige, his "Fifty-Three Stations of the Tokaido" and "A Hundred Scenes of Famous Edo Places" are perhaps the most reproduced series of woodblock prints in the *ukiyoe* tradition. In the late Seventies, the world's largest news daily, the *Yomiuri Shimbun,* issued both series as a monthly incentive to keep long-term subscribers.

In an unpublished report, an American scholar said he was shocked that the venerable scholars didn't understand what seemed obvious to him. He found their speculation that Hiroshige may have been playing a practical joke or trying to prevent counterfeits ludicrous. Although he jestingly suggested exhumation of Edo corpses to count toes, he insisted that the sixth lobe is not a toe.

Anyone can verify this by observing that without shoes, the foot normally widens out and continues to outline the pattern established by the toes. The sole pad beneath the little toe spreads out with similar dimensions. While Hiroshige and his contemporaries were influenced by shading and other techniques of Western engraving and

etching on copper plate, woodblock technology limited the detail to which shadowing and molded shading could be done. Further, done with the speed Hiroshige must have employed to be so productive, it would be inevitable that the outline would become deceptive.

Close observation of hand-painted works a century before Hiroshige turns up similar instances where the footpad resembles a toe, especially in illustrations that fail to delineate toenails.

Most collections of *ukiyoe* see the light of day only once in a decade or so. In order to further preserve the original colors, many can be seen only under dim, artificial light that makes it impossible to see the original color anyway. Still there are enough collections available in and out of Japan (Boston is best) where you can always go and see this phenomenon for yourself.

If your interest is no deeper than the average Japanese, it is at least possible to look interested. You don't have to tell anyone you are counting toes, *or* you can one-up everyone by demonstrating how thoroughly you know more than the Japanese. You can keep your shoes on. . . .

As if to add injury to insult, in an apparently handmade enlargement the Yomiuri collection's folder illustration splits a big toe as if to positively demonstrate modern Japanese are out of touch with their artistic tradition. . . . Could the copyist be unfamiliar with *geta,* or could they be looking for copyright protection?

Why *Haiku?*

The popularity of *haiku* is easy to explain: whole poems are shorter than just one of Shakespeare's couplets. Why, even foreigners who never studied Japanese can translate them. Further, they can write their own *haiku,* presumably in the style of Bashō, or at least inspired by him. (Just try a Shakespearean sonnet of your own, or a couplet even). Worldwide quotability and an apparent ease of imitation ensure Bashō gets the highest form of flattery. Whether he would see it as such is another question.

So is Japanese appreciation of Bashō. Universal familiarity with Bashō's frog may not breed contempt, but does not make Froggy popular, either. The smiles of appreciation and tones of admiration you experience upon mentioning Froggy are for *you*, not Bashō. While every schoolchild has a brush with Bashō in dreaded homework, they are unaware of his world-class status. Thus your coming up with the *haiku* equivalent of "To be or not to be . . ." evokes a reaction which you can only see as appropriate for the work, hardly your erudition.

The fact is, however, *haiku* at the popular level is old-fashioned, stilted, loaded with clichés and obscure allusions of a near Biblical character. Never mind the small minority of contemporary writers who have broken away from the 5-7-5 syllable structure — they're just young intellectuals without an outlet for their social consciences. Any way you slice it, there is none of the "kerplunk" found in English "translations" ground out almost as fast as the self-styled translator can find the words in the Japanese-English dictionary he happened to stumble across in his college library. Instead of worrying about whether to give "plop," "splash" or what have you for what in the original is literally "the sound of water," surely it would be easier to compose your own *haiku*.

Literary scholarship that can translate without knowledge of Japanese is so common a stereotype that even hilariously blatant parodies of it can deceive the Japanese public. Is this part of the inclination to expect all *gaijin* not to be able to speak Japanese?

But even when short poems are written in English along the 5-7-5 syllable pattern, they still have more in common with e.e. cummings or Ogden Nash than with Bashō or Issa. A "syllable" counting system whereby Yokohama, Osaka, Nippon and the Japanized form of "frog" (furoggu) all have four syllables is beyond the genius of English.

Furthermore, the materials available in English carry none of the moldiness of Japanese tradition and have a freshness similar to Shakespeare in modern Japanese translation.

While something may be gained in the translation, it certainly wasn't — or isn't — in the original. Thus, while Bashō might not entirely disapprove of what is produced in English, he would hardly consider it real *haiku*.

Why *Ikebana?*

Ikebana is usually translated as "the art of flower arrangement." The qualifying "Japanese" is often added to this, and quite rightly so. Other countries hardly see the necessity to make the arrangement of dying flowers into an art form. Not that it is really an original Japanese idea, having originated in India and developed hand-in-hand with that other dubious art form, the Tea Ceremony.

As a form worth studying, perfecting and copying, however, it became curiously Japanese in form and so it remains today. It is certainly an art form — the not-so-gentle art of making money and conning people. In fact the seriousness with which it is regarded by its devotees puts it almost akin to a religion, with its own strict hierarchy and its constant pursuit of enlightenment. Its growing popularity in other countries only proves how good the Japanese are at persuading others that the mysterious Orient is alive and well and worth copying, with its frugality and subtlety of expression. Of course it is popular — the world is full of unoriginal people who can't even put flowers in a bowl artistically.

In Japan itself, the *ikebana* fanatics do take it very seriously. But their belief in it is not for the purest reasons. It is a very material passion at all levels. The humble student tends to study it because a certificate always looks good, and it is something one traditionally should do as preparation for marriage and all that. Keep at it and you might one day rise to the dizzy ranks of *sensei*.

Now, why do the *sensei* do it? It is not only for altruistic reasons, dare it be said. They are, of course, passing on the Word to the flower people, but couldn't that be done in about 10 minutes? All you have to do is distinguish Heaven, Man and Earth and tell other people that the way they do it naturally is incorrect. But money is involved, too.

Money for what? Money to get your certificate. That's why nobody ever complains about it. You see, you can play with flowers in the company of others, which is more exciting than studying English, you can become a teacher yourself, and then you can start charging the earth, man and heaven to your own students. One of the most rewarding jobs ever, and it looks pretty.

Well, that needs qualification. It did look pretty, until the likes of Sogetsu started introducing plastics, wires, dolls and all that kind of nonsense, thus trying to prove that it is an art form of infinite variety, capable of branching out into the abstract. This was, however, something of a necessity, making it possible for many different ''schools'' to co-exist, each possessing a tenuous ''originality.''

But, all things considered, perhaps it is ultimately a creative thing, still concerned with the pursuit of beauty. And if you want to be an artist, but have no real artistic pretensions, then it is the art form for you, especially if you keep it as simple as possible and stick to flowers and grasses — certainly, nobody will ever say they dislike your arrangement, except the teachers, of course. That's why you pay them.

Why *Bonsai?*

Sorry to bore you with a theme you must have heard repeated a thousand times if you've heard it once, but the Japanese have a very special relationship with nature. They love nature, especially if it doesn't take up too much room and can be sold for an enormous profit. This is true of nature's tiniest creatures — summer insects trapped in little matchstick cages and sold to schoolboys for a month's pocket money. And it is equally true of nature's greatest giants — trees. Trees cannot be trapped and caged, but they can be trimmed, pruned and stunted down to a fraction of their natural size; and then the right tree can be sold, not to a schoolboy for ¥500 or so, but to a retired politician for an amount equivalent to the average *salaryman's* summer bonus. It's enough to make anyone fall in love with nature.

Bonsai literally means "tray-growing," and that's just what it is: things that look like fully grown trees but are only six inches high and growing in a shallow dish. Growing them requires patient pruning and cruel clipping, and usually the application of strong wires and other apparati for forcing the tree to grow in a more natural appearance than it would if permitted to grow naturally. The impression of natural size is further enhanced if you make a whole "garden" in the dish: a miniature shrine perhaps, or at least a couple of pebbles carefully chosen to look like huge rocks. Next time you watch a classic of the Japanese cinema, try to guess how many of those magnificent vistas of misty scenery were really *bonsai,* filmed on the director's kitchen table, with the mist added to hide the teacups, ashtrays and tomato ketchup bottles.

All this macho mastery of the giants of nature has an air of brutal domination about it, and so is a favorite hobby among men, who look down in scorn on something like *ikebana,* which is mere fiddling about with sissy flowers, not real, big trees.

Never confuse *bonsai* with *Banzai!* The *gaijin* is not rare who has had to leave the company in disgrace, after shouting, *"Shacho bonsai!"* at the *shacho's* birthday party. Calling your boss a dwarf instead of wishing him ten thousand years of life is hardly the right road to rapid promotion.

Why Tea?

A Tea Ceremony is a moment of refined delicate elegance in an otherwise frenetic world. Its rules and techniques are a combination of Chinese practices, medieval loving-cup rituals and 18th century coffee-house gatherings. Indeed the English Tea Ceremony, consisting of less rigid rules and more real conversation, nevertheless retains the basic elements of ritual, with the addition of cucumber sandwiches.

Like so many surviving traditions, the *chanoyu* began amongst the élite, who delighted in stressing the simplicity of real refinement, and it still retains that aura of respectability. It's a fairly harmless pursuit, really, unfortunately endowed with rather an overdose of that hypocritical politeness which may achieve superficial harmony, but little else:

"I must apologize for the terrible quality of this miserable tea bought at only ¥4,000 a packet. I must also apologize for following the great master Sen-no-Rikyu's instructions to the letter and providing tea-bowls of the most simple design and no intrinsic value. This one, for example, a family heirloom dating back to the 16th century, is really unworthy to be placed before you."

"Oh, but it's lovely!"

"No, I really should have found one more suitable for the occasion."

"Oh, I've dropped it. I'm terribly sorry."

"No need to worry. That's why we invented *tatami,* after all! It's only worth a mere ¥5 million anyway. Another bowl?"

"Oh, yes please. That delightful, mouth-watering essence of green pea soup is so refreshing, especially to counteract the disgusting sickliness of these funny little cakes, or are they biscuits?"

"So glad you like them. I have them handmade in Kyoto and delivered every week. Such a nice little man makes them. Remind me to give you his number. Really very reasonable — much cheaper than English lessons."

"And so much more satisfying!"

Relaxation, false smiles and social oiling, that's what it's all about. Long may it go on, as it has done for centuries.

But just a moment. What is that? A new development? Yes, enter from stage left the new, dynamic "coffee ceremony.'' Taste buds and ears around the world prick up. What is it?

Originating, as one would expect, in Osaka, it's another of those very simple ideas which should have been tried ages ago. Someone realized two very important things: most people, especially foreigners, do not actually like the taste of *matcha*; and coffee consumption is increasing daily. Put those two things together, and add the fact that there are millions of Europeans drinking coffee out of bowls already, and you have the Coffee Ceremony.

This remains remarkably similar to the Tea Ceremony in outward appearance. Months, if not years of training are required to actually get that water through the filter in the appropriately elegant fashion, and everyone still oohs and aahs at the beauty of the thing. But it has the advantage that you can make a tedious Nescafé chore into something aesthetically satisfying and also try any kind of coffee you fancy. A brilliant idea which will no doubt sweep the world in years to come, and prove just how adaptive and international the Japanese are. Full marks for a great idea. Even better if they added fruitcake.

Why Zen on *Zabuton?*

Not only priests. Most Zenophiles. Which really makes it a very appealing religious activity: no sermons, no necessity to chat with the rest of the congregation, no need to shake hands with the vicar, etc., etc. And, you can sit on a cushion. Now just think of the ever-increasing popularity of Zen. Could there be a connection?

Zen doesn't believe in luxuries, however. It is clean, to the point, and in its purest forms involves a regime even worse than the Foreign Legion. It gives real devotees the chance to find themselves and the true nature of nature, human and otherwise, by way of frozen temples and occasional beatings to keep one awake — a kind of enlightenment through self-discipline and pain.

But it also displays that subtle flaw, that crack in the otherwise perfect cup, that deliberate mistake without which there is no perfection — a cushion to sit on.

This is truly the stroke of a master, because there is nothing else whatever cushy about Zen. Its riddles are nebulous and its demands are ethereal, but you do not have to spend half your life sitting on rocks under a waterfall, developing arthritis on highly polished floors or even pins and needles on *tatami* mats — there is the chance of a cushion.

Now that is definitely an improvement on the conditions suffered by more natural exponents of Zen: cows sitting in wet fields, crocodiles perenially meditating in muddy streams, and praying mantises forever pleading to heaven while stuck on a concrete wall.

But why do humans need a cushion for meditating? Is it that the pain and discomfort ensuing from never using one would really detract from emptiness of mind? Or is it some secret pact with the Zabuton Manufacturers' Association of Japan, which undoubtedly exists somewhere in the back streets of Nara? Or is it just a ploy to encourage more people to join the ranks? No, obviously not. According to one distinguished "primate," atop a thick mat, a small, round meditation cushion is placed, and one sits on that. An ordinary cushion doubled over may be used instead. Meditation takes place with the rear of the buttocks on this cushion, or even a chair is permissible.

So that's it. We've finally got to the bottom of the problem: it's the buttocks. How silly not to have noticed before. The human anatomy is not perfect for the *zazen* position.

However, that still begs the question of why it must be a cushion, rather than, say, a piece of wood rather like a geisha pillow?

But one thing is certainly clear: as soon as you start asking questions about Zen, you have to keep asking more questions about the questions, until the whole thing becomes a complicated Zen *mondo* in itself:

"Why do Zen priests sit on a *zabuton?*"

"What is the last letter of the alphabet?"

Glossary

This Glossary includes those Japanese expressions considered not to have been sufficiently explained in the text. They are mostly reproduced in what has become the most common transliteration for everyday purposes; other forms exist, with varying degrees of phonological accuracy. The decision which words to italicize, and which words not to italicize because they are already loanwords in English was difficult, and this book does not claim to be consistent or prescriptive in that respect. These glossary definitions are all true, except for one silly comment about *nattō*. The rest, it is hoped, will dispel some illusions about the complexity, perverseness, uniqueness and so many other features that have been claimed for the Japanese language.

A

Ah, raisu desuka? ああ、ライスですか。 Oh, is that rice? Oh, you mean rice?

Ah, sō desuka? ああ、そうですか。 Oh, is that so? Uncannily similar to German ''Ach, so?''

aikidō 合気道 a martial art, for self-defense only, of course

akachōchin 赤ちょうちん a kind of tavern for uninhibited eating and drinking, named for the red lantern hanging outside

anata あなた analogous to French or Spanish formal second person, derived from the more removed, formally polite ''anokata,'' hence a third person referent for ''you.'' But now used mostly by lovers and foreigners. Contrasts with less removed ''omae,'' ''kimi.''

arigatō gozaimashita ありがとうございました thank you — in the past tense, so: thank you for having come, bought something, etc.

arimasen ありません verb of existence + polite negative form: there isn't any; none are present. A standard way to say no; seems objective to the Japanese mind, so not thought of as saying ''no.''

ashi 脚・足 leg and/or foot, hence ''You have long feet,'' addressed to a tall person

B

bājin rōdo バージンロード Look carefully, and you'll see it's "virgin road." Self-explanatory.

banzai バンザイ literally, 10,000 years of life. Long live. . .! Viva. . .!

Bashō 芭蕉 Haiku poet (1644-1694), born Matsuo Munefusa, but used the name Basho, which means banana. With a name like that, he'd have to be a poet.

Beikoku 米国 America. Reasons for using the characters "rice country" are too complex to go into here.

benjo 便所 literally, "convenient place," originally euphemistic but now rather low word for lavatory

bentō 弁当 boxed lunch of rice garnished with meat, fish, vegetables and unidentifiables

bushidō 武士道 the traditional samurai code. Like chivalry, a useful excuse for being kind to animals and committing wartime atrocities.

C

chanoyu 茶の湯 the Tea Ceremony

cock-san コックさん a cook. From the Dutch "kok," so not so funny as it seems.

curry-rice カレーライス bears a slight resemblance to real curry

D

daimyō 大名 feudal lord. Literally, "big name," which he was.

daruma だるま gnomish doll, a talisman for success. Paint in one eye to pray for it, the other when it comes.

dekinai できない can't be done; impossible

depāto デパート department store, clipped short for convenience

E

ebi エビ shrimp, prawn

ebiburger エビバーガー burger of above, but with how much real ebi in it?

Edokko 江戸っ子 born-and-bred central Tokyo native, the Cockney of Japan

Eigo 英語 the English language. One of the meanings of the Ei- bit happens to be "hero," but that is not intended as a compliment to the English.

eikaiwa 英会話 English conversation

enka 演歌 modern Japanese songs, crooned or bawled from a part of the throat undiscovered in the West

F

furoshiki ふろしき cloth used for carrying things in the days before supermarket plastic bags. Foreigners use them as tablecloths, scarves, wall-hangings, etc.

G

gaijin 外人 "outside-person," and so a foreigner. A loanword to resident foreigners within a fortnight. Not a term of abuse, but felt as one by some.

gairaigo 外来語 vocab. imported and distorted to suit Japanese pronunciation, orthography, fashion and fancy

geta げた wooden clogs, with or without high blocks to keep the feet from the street

giri 義理 a position of debt, where you owe someone a favor

gohan ご飯 boiled rice in a bowl ready for eating or, by extension, any meal

gokiburi ゴキブリ appropriately creepy-crawly word for a cockroach

gomi ゴミ garbage, rubbish, trash

gyōza ギョーザ little Chinese-style pies stuffed with meat and enough garlic to clear a space around you in the train

H

haiku 俳句 literally "actor" + "phrase." Conventions of the Japanese language do not make direct quotes possible, so the term suggesting dramatic lines makes sense. Related terms that cause some confusion even for Japanese include "haikai" — which logically should apply to what is known as "senryu," but popularly used to indicate the genre as a whole. Its narrow usage refers to linked poems, usually humorous, composed by groups at parties.

hanamichi 花道 the "flower way," a passage through audience to the stage. Processions seem to take ages to cover what is really quite a short distance.

hanko ハンコ personal seal, name-stamp or chop

haramaki 腹巻 literally ''belly-winder,'' and that's what it is; ancient underwear, also useful for concealing money and other valuables

harō ハロー presumably ''Hello!'' A guide to contemporary usage gives this as a transliteration of ''hallo'' or ''halo.'' Take your pick.

hiragana ひらがな flowing script of syllables, nearly all consonant + vowel, representing only sound, no meaning

I

ijime いじめ bullying, harassment. For a while it was thought to be unique to Japanese schools, with no appropriate English term. Of course it is not only in schools.

ine 稲 rice still growing in the paddy fields

irasshaimase いらっしゃいませ Welcome! In shops, please come in and spend!

itadakimasu いただきます like ''bon appetit'' in French at the beginning of a meal. Untranslatable to English speakers, who just grab.

J

jidai 時代 age, dynasty, era, period, time etc.

jidai-matsuri 時代祭 the Festival of Ages, an annual festival in Kyoto for centuries

jinja 神社 shrine; distinguished from temples of Buddhist origin with the institution of the Imperial cult or Shinto, ''way of the gods.''

jinrikisha 人力車 literally man-power-cart, the origin of ''rickshaw.'' One of modern Japan's first inventions.

jūdō 柔道 a martial art, international since the Tokyo Olympics

juku 塾 cram school to push kids up the educational ladder. Nowadays there are even classes for kindergarten entrance.

K

kanji 漢字 written characters of Chinese origin. Each has one or more meanings, and one or more pronunciations. Sometimes called ideograms or pictograms.

karaoke カラオケ empty + orchestra (abbr.), taped song-music for bar customers to sing the words to and gain applause from the hostess

karate 空手 a martial art. Not everyone in Japan has a black belt.

katakana カタカナ angular version of hiragana. Mostly used for foreign and/or scientific words.

katakori 肩こり stiff shoulders

kattobase かっ飛ばせ Smash it! Slam it!!

kawaii かわいい cute. An overdone catchword.

kawaii-ko かわいい子 cute little girl, but usually it's just an act

kōban 交番 a police box, a small hut with a red (!!??) light for the local cops

kōhai 後輩 someone a year or more below at school, company, jail etc., to be treated with spite and cruelty by his senpai

kokeshi こけし small painted dolls resembling clothespins or bowling pins

kokoro 心 heart. An overused word emotively referring to mind, spirit, friendship, kindness, etc.

kome 米 polished rice ready to be used for cooking, but not cooked yet

kuroko 黒子 theater assistant rendered theoretically invisible by a black hood

M

manga 漫画 cartoons, comics

matcha 抹茶 thick, bitter, green Tea Ceremony tea

mimi 耳 This word means ear(s), although it looks like a good name for a French poodle.

misoshiru 味噌汁 soup with a miso (bean-paste) base. Despite its high salt content, it's popular with Western health-food freaks.

momi もみ Most dictionaries say rice in the husks, but. . . .

momo 桃 peach, peaches. A near homophone is ''thighs,'' differing only in which syllable gets higher pitch — a distinction which does not prevent the usual punning.

mondō 問答 a question-and-answer session, catechism. In Zen, both Q and A try hard to be enigmatic.

N

nai ない (there is) not/no. . . . Technically a verbal adjective, colloquially similar to ''ain't.''

naruhodo なるほど Now it's clear! Ah, I see!

nattō 納豆 fermented soy beans that some, but not all, Japanese claim to be delicious. Uniquely Japanese, so unpalatable to foreigners.

nengō 年号 year number in an era, based more or less on an emperor's reign. Showa is the longest ever.

Nihon/Nippon 日本 Japan in Japanese. With a -pp- it's a bit more patriotic.

Nihongo 日本語 the Japanese language. Foreigners learn this, while the Japanese learn another one, called Kokugo (national language).

ninja 忍者 highly athletic samurai spy able to become invisible. Ideal for TV dramas.

nozoki のぞき peeping, and all that that implies

O

o- お the honorific, sometimes also go- or mi- or on-. Anyone who translates it as "honorable" is just being silly.

obi 帯 not only a kimono sash, but also the one round a book or record

o-cha お茶 tea. With the honorific, always green tea as served in offices, police boxes, etc.

o-furo お風呂 a bath

o-kaasan おかあさん mother. Despite the honorific, frequently downtrodden.

o-miai お見合い meeting with a view to arranging a marriage. The -ai bit has nothing to do with the word for love.

on 恩 a position of credit, where someone owes you a favor

o-nigiri おにぎり a rice ball, wrapped in seaweed and with a little filling inside to make it palatable

onnagata 女形 a male performer of female roles, often famous and highly honored

P

pachinko パチンコ onomatopoeic name for pinball popular with university students and gangsters

patokā パトカー Look carefully, and you'll see it's a shortened form of "patrol car," which is what it means.

R

raisu ライス rice on a plate, ready to eat

rāmen ラーメン Chinese noodles of a type unknown in China

rōmaji ローマ字 the letters of the Roman alphabet, especially as used for producing unreadable versions of Japanese

ryokan 旅館 literally "travel" + "lodge," a travelers' inn with traditional setting and emphasis on privacy (in contrast to hotels or minshuku)

S

salaryman サラリーマン a Japanglish invention with an obvious meaning, that has no equivalent in English. More correctly sarariman.

samurai サムライ ancient feudal warrior, who would do anything for his lord and anything to his subordinates

-san さん appended to a person's name with the effect of Mr., Mrs., Ms., etc. Used freely with other titles, company names, etc. Never use it for yourself.

satsuma imo さつま芋 the sweet potato, introduced into Satsuma in S. Kyushu. Known in Japan for the same digestive effect as baked beans in Boston or Birmingham. Its distilled spirits taste like spoiled tequila.

sazan island サザンアイランド The bottle will tell you it's "Thousand Island," although it looks more like "Southern Island." Ask the waitress if she knows which it is.

senpai 先輩 anybody senior to you, opposite of kōhai; must be accorded great respect

shabu-shabu しゃぶしゃぶ sliced beef cooked at the table in a pan of water; similar to sukiyaki, but different

shachō 社長 company president; term of flattery used by con-men

shiatsu 指圧 literally finger-pressure, a type of massage

shikataganai しかたがない there's no way; can't be done, or the like

shimbun 新聞 literally new hearing, a newspaper

Shinkansen 新幹線 literally, and rather uninspiringly, new trunk line; the bullet train

shita した/下/舌 completed form of the verb to do, or "below," or "tongue." Needlessly confused by the absence of the first form in dictionaries, and the practice of teaching only the polite form "shimashita" to foreigners. English-Japanese dictionaries give entries for all forms.

shiti シティ transliteration for city. It takes on an additional meaning many English speakers accept as unfortunately accurate.

shōchū 焼酎 (pure) distilled spirits usually from 20 to 35 percent alcohol. Sources and popularity vary.

soba そば usually translated as buckwheat noodles, which doesn't help much; brownish grey Japanese-style noodles *sukiyaki* すき焼 famous traditional meal, mostly eaten by foreigners. Suki- has nothing to do with the word that means "I like it."

sumō 相撲 wrestling performed by huge men called behemoths or burly grapplers by journalists desperate for an apt description

sumōtori 相撲取り behemoth, burly grappler

supeido スペード transliteration of English "spade" — both suit in cards and shovel, but nothing to do with spayed cats

T

taruzake 樽酒 sake from new cypress or cedar kegs, usually drunk cold from square wooden cups, often with salted corner rims. Some insist it is better than Greek retsina or ordinary sake. Others insist that is not really praise.

tatami 畳 rush mats for eating, sleeping, doing everything on except wearing slippers

tera 寺 temple from Buddhist tradition. When prefixed with a name, the T is often voiced as D.

tomesode 留袖 literally "stopped sleeves," kimono worn by married women. The sleeves are shorter than on an unmarried maiden's — to make washing up easier?

U

umeboshi 梅干し little salted, pickled plums eaten to give rice a little taste, usually dyed red. To be approached with care by the uninitiated.

Y

Yomiuri 読売 literally "reading" + "selling," something like "Post and Dispatch." The company publishes the world's largest daily newspaper, and owns Japan's winningest baseball team, a TV network, department stores, etc.

yukata 浴衣 casual kimono

Z

zabuton 座ぶとん a cushion on the floor

zazen 座禅 Zen meditation on the floor